Forget the Urgent!

Rather Focus on the Important

by

Matías Birrell & Javier Arévalo

First edition © 2012
ISBN   978-1481249034 (printed edition)

Authors:
Matías Birrell Rodríguez
Javier Arévalo Jiménez

Edited by Henry Camp

Preface

In the introduction to the first edition of "The Goal" in 1984, Dr. Goldratt wrote:

"The Goal" is about *New* global principles of manufacturing".

We believe that Theory of Constraints is about *New* global principles of management for any organization. The best summary of these principles is contained in the introduction Dr. Goldratt wrote for a book that he could not finish under the title "The Science of Management" and (hopefully for a long time) it will be found in internet:

http://www.youtube.com/watch?v=iFYoPqcTy3Y

The characters of this book are fictional; however they reflect many real interactions that the authors have experienced through the years, in many companies of several countries. Our encounter with Goldratt Theory and with Eli Goldratt himself (he did not like us to call him doctor) was of similar fashion. A close friend and colleague in the companies we worked around 1996-97, separately, recommended us we read a book: "The Goal". At first, it shocked us since it flew against conventional practice, but it was conventional wisdom... common sense. We were hooked as we saw the lines in the book describing our issues and the problems we faced in each of our jobs at the time. We had the audacity (maybe being naïve) to put the book principles to practice in our best understanding. It worked! Beyond our belief, much simpler than what we were used to. Few years later, as we, the authors, met for the first time, when TOC brought us together with like interests, we had the incredible fortune to not only meet Eli, but as we independently had decided to build our expertise and knowledge further, we came to work closely with him for several years before his passing. This was a life changing experience. We received in Eli a teacher, mentor and a friend.

This book is our humble way of paying homage to the person and the mentor we had in Eli, and hoping that it will serve the purpose to stimulate any person and the readers to embark on a road of discovery and self improvement. It is a challenging road full of rewards, the way to lead a meaningful life.

The invitation to forget the urgent in our life is not suggesting an irresponsible attitude of neglecting important issues. This book is about very simple principles to manage organizations in a way that allows managers to keep control, avoiding the danger of the urgent driving a continuous improvisation, with a reactive mode of operation instead of a much better proactive one.

Matías Birrell & Javier Arévalo
Santiago de Chile, November 2012

I

I am between a rock and a hard place.

This week I have been working hard, staying late at my desk, trying to make progress in all the important issues that I cannot deal with when I am surrounded by people asking for resolutions in many and vastly different areas of the company. Yes, I am the man.

It is 8:30 pm Thursday and looking at my list of top priorities, I see that I have more than when I came to the office on Monday. Yes, all of them are important. And now, it seems that many of them are also urgent.

I feel as if I'm drowning in the urgent. I try hard to get out but it is inevitable that more important issues turn urgent as I go about solving the old urgent ones. The problem with urgent issues is precisely that, they are urgent and need immediate attention. I try to understand what urgent means.

Let's see. If I ignore even one of them, the future consequences will be significantly negative. That is the meaning of important. When the "future" is now or very close, then it is also urgent.

I look at my list again. I would like to believe that I can end the week with fewer urgent things to do. At least that would provide me with a sense of productivity. Today I feel as if I have wasted most of the week. I know that I should take care of the important aspects of the strategy but I have only been able to touch them on the surface, always interrupted by the urgent. At this pace it will take forever, in other words, we are fooling ourselves that we have a strategic plan for the next years.

I recognize my ability to make fast decisions in difficult situations. I know others recognize that ability in me as well. My position as CEO was confirmed last month after four years. All the employees seem to recognize it, too, because they keep coming with their problems.

Problems. Do I understand what a problem is? Many times I cannot understand why someone comes to me with such so-called problems when I can solve them in a minute.

Many other times I face real problems. Those that appear, I solve them, and after a while, weeks or months later, they appear again. I have tried many different solutions, optimizing this and that, but whatever decision I make it seems that I create a source for another problem.

And my list of important issues is always plagued by the urgent.

I know that we are good. The company has been growing at a good pace and profitability is more than acceptable.

But I also know that if I only could manage to implement all the good ideas that our management team has for the different areas, the company could do much better. I don't fool myself thinking that this is good enough. It is not for me. It is only a matter of time before the competitors catch up and do what we have been planning.

Even if they don't, I don't like working so hard, stealing time from my family, for a fairly good result. There must be a way out. I don't see it.

I am between a rock and a hard place. I better go home now.

II

It's Friday morning. At 7:00 I am still alone, I can review my emails peacefully. I wonder why they keep on sending all that spam. Some of it is definitely undesirable, plus all the viruses, trojans and scams.

Today there is one email that catches my eye, it was forwarded by a close friend. Some of those could qualify as spam as well. Usually I wouldn't pay attention to those 'you-can't-miss-it' messages, but today it is especially irritating. It is like the author is laughing at me, as if he could have read my mind last night. "Fwd: Forget the urgent!" I resist a little bit more the temptation of opening it. Well, I can lose fifteen seconds.

"The urgent has only three sources: poor empowerment, or an important thing was delayed too much, or a surprise caught you unprepared."

This seems too obvious. I must admit that five minutes ago I would have said that the urgent has many sources. I can tell: all the people in my company, more than two hundred souls!

Right, that statement is absolutely correct and it wasn't obvious at all. Would it be of any help now to solve my constant problem?

"Learn how TOC (Theory of Constraints) can help eliminating the three sources of the urgent! Allow yourself to focus on the important!"

Whoa, I knew it! It is just another three letter acronym to sell a book, seminar or coaching. That was close!

"Find out how to discover the root cause to all your urgencies, all of them stem from the same core conflict."

Okay, enough! I've got work to do.

It is not that bad. There are only eleven new real messages, on top of the twenty two that are still pending. My list has only seven more issues. I believe that prioritizing them (again) would be the first step. I guess that the most important issue is to produce the cash for the bills that are due this week, and then reviewing the marketing plan that was submitted for approval, or I better look into that proposal for a new warehouse system. I wonder how long it will take for finance to produce the calculations I asked for to decide on the discounts that two of our salesmen are asking for.

Of course all these issues came to me after careful consideration by the manager of the area. Still, I know by experience how biased an area manager can be, taking care of his silo. I can't afford approving decisions over certain amount without proper analysis. The devil is always in the details!

Each one of these things need time and thinking. Although I would like to believe that all of them stem from only one cause, I don't see how that would be possible in my case. I must admit that the idea is very appealing – only one cause for all my concerns. If I can solve it, that would narrow my list considerably!

What was the name of that thing? TOC, theory of constraints. A fast search in Google gives me more than four and a half million results. Apparently, TOC was originated more than thirty years ago by an Israeli physicist, Dr. Eliyahu Goldratt. So at least this is not the last flavor of the month. I read more and his most famous book is "The Goal". A physicist in business? Interesting, I may take a look at that book some time.

I have my MBA and all my management team does, too. I look around and I haven't heard of any brilliant idea that could solve this vicious cycle of delaying important things turning them urgent, which in turn delay more important things.

I haven't heard of such a bold claim in any other time management course or seminar. At most, there you find good ideas to prioritize tasks.

Now that I think of it, prioritizing is only required when I can't do everything within a reasonable timeframe. Most of my tasks are not due immediately; in fact most of them wait several days, even weeks. Then, prioritizing is the fancy word for choosing what tasks will turn urgent or will be dismissed (these are the ones that looked important but they weren't, but how to know in advance).

I know why I'm trapped in this vicious cycle. It is because I can't ignore all the important issues in my list. Even the article "The magic of doing one thing at a time" recently appeared in HBR about bad multitasking sounds full of good intentions but with very little practicality in my case. I simply can't avoid the constant shift between tasks because the urgency of them demands my immediate attention.

What could it be that one thing that solves it all? It sounds like fantasy.

It is almost 7:30 now, so I must finish something before the day starts with the unavoidable vicious cycle.

III

The bank was more than pleased to extend us an additional line of credit. We solved the problem this month, but we need to reduce our inventories that are tying up so much cash. The last time that we made an inventory reduction across the board, we soon were short of three raw materials. That was enough to stop one of our lines for two days. It was clear that time that the reduction was much more expensive than the recovered cash, without even considering the extra cost of the urgent shipment for the missing materials.

That was the same conclusion we came to each of the seven times in the last five years when we found ourselves forced to reduce inventories to produce cash. Now it is different. With the new forecasting system that we bought, we should have much more clarity of our future needs so the inventory reduction should be safe. Or so I hope.

Part of the problem is that our warehouses are packed. In the last weeks we have been storing items in different places and sometimes they can't find them when they are needed. That's why we are considering a new warehouse management system (WMS).

All the proposals are for WMS software designed for retail distribution centers and huge amount of items. Of course we could benefit from using such gorgeous pieces of technology, but not at this price. We are manufacturers. We have two warehouses, one for raw materials and the other for finished goods.

I don't want to make the same mistakes that we did with the ERP. Finally, it cost us a fortune, consumed much too much of our time for months to implement it, and I haven't seen real benefits in the bottom line after three years, in spite of all the benefits that we put together in the last presentation for the board. Honestly, those questions regarding the impact on profit or investment were especially irritating because I myself knew that there were no good bottom line results. Apparently shareholders do not like soft results.

Back to the inventory reduction, I guess that it would be much better if the emphasis is in the finished goods. I know that the new promotion program, which is part of the marketing plan that I have to approve, will necessitate a lot of inventory. Well, they will have to do with seventy percent of what they asked for. I know how it is; these estimates contain a lot of safety in them.

We must plan this reduction carefully. We don't want to starve the plant. Our production cost would climb and our competitiveness would suffer. I better make sure that sales department increases the volumes, so that more products leave our warehouse while we still are producing at a reasonable cost.

That shouldn't be hard to do. I know what shortages are at the points of sale. I believe that I will (strongly) suggest that our sales manager recruits the help of the operations manager, to use our new forecasting system and apply it with our clients. I'm sure they should appreciate such innovative and sophisticated service. Now we could really help them deciding on the quantities per order. This is going to be a hit.

Clients never liked when we suggested how much they should buy before. They think that we want to get rid of our surplus. Yes, we do, but through solving their shortages. I hope that the new system will build the trust to make this work in a win-win relationship. I really want to make good, but cannot forget that I also have a problem to solve.

IV

After three weeks, I am still not sure about the investment in the new WMS. Stocks have gone down by 15%. Not even a single client accepted our offer of using our forecasting system to help them with the ordering. Instead, several accepted increasing the orders for a 5% discount. Now we have made some room in the finished goods warehouse, so I don't really see the need for a WMS now. The discounts wiped a good portion of the anticipated profit; I decide that I will not approve more investments for a while if I can help it.

The marketing plan was approved with a lesser adjustment to the stocks requested originally and ten percent less in the budget. I know that we need to invest in order to grow, but I need to take care of the current operation as well. I don't want to be asking for bank loans just to cover for well intended but not secured marketing campaigns.

Today I received the sales report for the last week. An alarming 25% decline will grab my attention for a while. My first thought is that this is a normal fluctuation of the market. We have observed this before, but my sales manager is worried because this month they could miss the quotas by more than 15%.

I try to imagine how it looks like for an external observer, from ten thousand feet above. We produce a wide range of low and middle price consumer products that we store at our warehouse. Our clients, wholesalers and distributors buy from us every week, and they sell to retailers.

Consumers come to the shops and buy our products. In a certain shop, a typical item is sold with a very fluctuating pattern. One day it is possible to sell five units while others only one, and others more than ten. That could explain the fluctuations.

But looking into it a little deeper, I can imagine that in a given day, one shop sells one item and another sells seven of the same item. If I consider all of the shops that are serviced by a distributor, the daily average should not be that fluctuating, because the quantities sold average out. And if I consider all the distributors and the wholesalers that I sell to, my weekly average should not fluctuate much. Definitely I wouldn't expect a 25% drop in a week. We are not at the end of a season, like Christmas.

This drop must have resulted from other causes. Most likely the sales force was content with the 12% increase two weeks ago and now they reduced the push to the clients. I better have a meeting with our commercial manager to understand better and recommend possible actions. I know there is room to grow.

Well, I guess that the sales meeting is more important than discussing the new product development methodology. I will postpone that one; I can't receive anyone this afternoon while we don't see how to increase sales again.

People really don't understand how complex this work is.

V

"Richard, hi. You don't have time for your friends anymore!"

I couldn't ignore again my cell phone and took the call from Bill, my dear friend that sends me those 'wise emails'. I guess that it's already late again, and we could relax together.

"Hi Bill, you know how it is, this is a never boring job".

"Don't tell me you are still working".

"Okay, I won't. What about a beer in twenty minutes?"

"Done".

One of the things that I like about driving late from work is that traffic has already softened. It takes me fifteen minutes to be seated and ask for two beers and chicken wings. If I know him, Bill will be here any minute now.

I remember when we were studying engineering, Bill was a good student and from time to time he surprised us with deep analyses. I thought that he would have a good career as an executive in big companies. However we soon knew his inclination was more for alternative paths; underground one could say may describe it better.

When he started investing time in this thing called TOC, I shared the same concern as two other of his friends. We believed that better he found a good job based on his past experience in executive positions, but Bill decided that this was what he wanted to do. He claimed that with TOC he would make a good living and besides he would be able to do something meaningful. I would know what he meant years later.

The "good living" didn't come for years and his case was one to clearly help understand the difference between 'stubbornness' and 'perseverance'. The perseverant has a goal.

As Bill arrives, so do the beers.

"Thank you, where are yours?" This joke is our tradition and I politely laugh. It's good to see friends are always kids.

"Hi Bill, good to see you in the country".

"Yeah, well, you know how it is. I have now two weeks with no trips so I can enjoy the family and maybe to do some sailing. What about you? Did you receive what I sent you?"

"Please, don't sell me now, I just wanted to enjoy a beer and get to know what happened lately with you".

"No problem, you see, for a few years now I have been doing only what I like and, better yet, they pay me for it. And I have a good deal of time every two weeks with all the family, besides all weekends, of course".

"I'm happy for you. It took you time to get here, it is only fair that you enjoy it now".

"Thanks. What can you tell me? I hope everything is fine at home and at work".

"At home it's the usual; the children are growing faster than one planned. Marcy thinks that I work too hard, I interpret her preoccupation as a complaint for not having more time together. At work I'm somehow content because everyone seems to be happy around me with our performance, but still..."

I'm not sure whether or not revealing some of my frustration to Bill will be a good idea. After all he would not miss the opportunity to play the consultant with me.

"But still...?"

Fine, venting with a friend is much better than with anyone else at home or at work.

"Look Bill, I don't say everything is perfect, all my friends in similar positions have problems. But isn't it that this capability of ours to solve problems is what makes us valuable to our companies?"

Bill raises his beer, I imitate him and he says laughing, "To the good managers that can juggle better than anyone else", and we finish our beers while I try to understand what part of that sarcasm was painful for me.

"What is it then? I know that there is something bothering you," Bill says more seriously.

"I received the message that you forwarded me and I admit that I was reflecting on this situation where I stand today. No matter how hard I try, I can't drain my list of urgencies. And I don't believe that there is a way out. Nobody is saying that but you and that TOC theory."

"So you don't believe that it is possible something just because a majority says so? You know better than that. Remember the genetic inheritance laws that we learned in basic biology?"

"I do. So?"

"Well, Mendel offered his theory to all scientists of his time and he was rejected or ignored by the majority. He even died before his laws were accepted, and now there is no doubt about the validity of those laws."

"What are you saying? Is this TOC theory comparable to that?"

"Well, Dr. Goldratt claimed to have found the unified field theory of management. As in physics, a theory like that would explain all the forces in the universe, which is not yet found but physicists consider it the philosopher's stone for their knowledge."

"If I'm not wrong, the philosopher's stone is a myth." There are so many management theories that every new inventor thinks that his is the panacea. The followers are usually worse.

"I don't blame you Richard, for caring about your time. I only say that perhaps you should listen a little bit more and judge by yourself. Anyway, no prophet was well received in his own land, right?"

"What does it mean?"

"Okay, this should be obvious, but I'll explain. For the last six years I have been well received and listened in hundreds of companies in other countries. I get paid because I deliver real value; I know how to do it. That should be enough for you, a friend, to give me some credit, but I understand the prejudices that you may have."

"Don't be a baby, stop crying, would you?"

"Good phrase, I may use it some time. So you were saying something about being content, but still…?"

"Yeah, right, but we don't have time now, I'd better get going now, it was good to see you again and I'm glad you're doing well my friend. We'll continue this conversation, I promise."

"I'm always ready for a beer when possible, please don't lose my number."

On my way home I reflect on what Bill told me. He may be right and I am not considering him at all to help me with my problem. But if I encourage him and finally I am not satisfied, that could hurt our friendship.

VI

The end of the quarter is always the same old story. Everything seems to be urgent. This time could be different, though. After the last marketing plan, a big portion of the inventories that we successfully sold to distributors with the promise of a strong and ample promotion in the points of sale is not yet sold. There is pressure from the big ones to return the excess.

They call it excess but I know that these goods will be sold eventually! The promotion was ample, and strong, and expensive. And it really increased sales, it's not my fault that they wouldn't buy more of the high runners! The big ones want to always win! I cannot afford to accept the returns in big volumes. Perhaps we could negotiate a partial return and only with the real important clients.

Sales increased. If I accept a big volume of returns, that figure will be decreased in the same amount that we will recognize the increase of inventories as current assets. For the balance sheet it will not be that bad... for now, until we must write them off or sell them at big discounts, but that is not a concern for the current quarter. The real hit will be in cash.

Besides, if I don't accept the returns, many of the clients have declared that they will reduce the purchase volume significantly during the next months. I must also take care of the medium and long term.

Yes, this time could be much worse than usual. 'From hero to zero in a snap'. What an injustice. And to make things worse,

Marcy doesn't seem to understand the problems that I have here and we've had more frequent fights lately.

I am sure that Bill couldn't deal with such pressure. TOC is probably a good theory for easy problems, the kind that most companies have, but not this crisis.

A full month has passed since our incomplete beer conversation. I guess that unless I try it, I won't know how Bill's theory could help. He seems to be too sure, maybe the benefit of the doubt applies here.

It's Friday and it's very likely that Bill will be in town. An sms will be enough.

VII

"Richard! How are you doing, man?"

This time Bill was earlier and asked for the traditional two beers and a good tartar with toasts.

"I've seen better days", I say while I sit.

"Hey, don't be a baby!", he says with a grin. I know that I deserve it.

"Look, the last weeks have been especially hard and I've been wondering how that theory of yours would help me. I have real problems and I don't want to regret not trying everything I have at hand." As Bill shows he understands, I continue, "I know the usual ain't working! I've tried it and I have this nagging feeling that I am running out of time, or at least running in circles."

"So the situation is that desperate that you ask me for help?" Bill says smiling as if the sarcasm could be less bitter, at least for me. "Just kidding, of course I want to show you the ways of TOC to deal with all those problems. But now let us relax and talk about our next sailing."

"Good idea, I need to clear and refresh my head. Anyway, when can you come and have a first look?" I don't want to let Bill block his scarce time in town without a firm commitment now that I decided to give him an opportunity.

"I will be here for two weeks, so there is plenty of time to complete a full analysis, what about tomorrow to start?"

That declaration was surprising. I doubt that all my problems could vanish in two weeks, but as I don't want to offend him, I say, "I agree."

VIII

The morning is cloudy but warm. I feel comfort in days like this one. Bill arrives sharp as always. He doesn't bring anything, not a laptop or even a pen.

"Hi Bill, what do you want, water, coffee, a soda?"

"A glass of water for me, thanks".

We get our drinks ourselves because on Saturdays there are no assistants. Back to the office we sit. I don't want to start without addressing my first concern.

"Bill, I appreciate that you came this morning and I know that I asked you to come. However I want to express a concern I have first."

"Sure, we can start with that one", he smiles.

"You know that I've been always skeptical about all the theories that claim to solve it all, so I want to tell you upfront that I want to have the liberty of stopping this and you will not be offended. Is this okay with you?"

Bill stands up. I wouldn't think he was so sensitive as to abandon with such little warning. But he takes a marker and goes to the board.

"So you want to protect our friendship and have your problems solved, both at the same time, do you agree?", he says as his writes these two statements one below the other and places a B and a C.

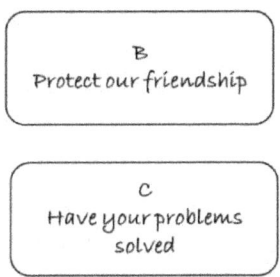

"Yes?", I don't know where this is going but I promised to cooperate.

He writes three more boxes with letters in them and reads aloud.

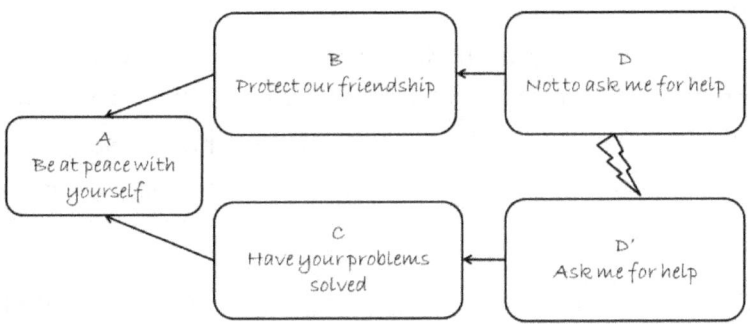

"On the one hand, to be at peace with yourself, you need to protect our friendship; and to protect our friendship you need not to ask me for help. Does it make sense?"

"Well, yes, although I might have chosen other words."

He ignores my remark and continues. "On the other hand, to be at peace with yourself, you need to have your problems solved; and to have your problems solved you need to ask me for help. Does this diagram express what you were afraid of?"

"I wasn't afraid of anything", I say instinctively.

"Okay, something was bothering you, is this close enough?"

"Yes, I'd say it is well put, but you would understand that I had my reasons to be reluctant." I don't want to offend him just starting.

"I fully understand it, Richard. Don't you see that I have put myself in your shoes and saw the conflict you were caught in?"

"What conflict? I was just reluctant." I don't like the words Bill is using: fear, conflict, as if I can't deal with problems. I am in this position because I have demonstrated my capabilities, and done well at it. These fears and conflicts have nothing to do with it... I know how to make decisions..., I know how to solve conflicts... I am not afraid... I feel a little bit upset now. I will allow this to continue for a while but I sadly see that my suspicions were true. Now I need to bear with Bill for a morning at least to avoid the conflict.

"Richard, what I just described is the best definition of your concern, isn't it?"

"Yes, but –"

"Let me finish, please." I must admit that I'm curious. I keep quiet.

"The diagram that I've just showed you is what we, in TOC, call the 'conflict cloud', and it is a logical diagram that depicts the black and white of a problem. Would you have defined your uneasiness about this first conversation in other terms?"

"I'm not used to complicated diagrams to express simple things. I told you what my concern was; that's all." I must admit that he has a point. Before this diagram I just had a bad feeling, but now it is clear. "But yes, I see how the problem is properly defined now."

"Richard, I understand the effort that this exercise can mean to you and I appreciate it. Please, consider that a solution is only required when there is a problem. Shall we continue?"

"Sure, now that you've defined the problem, how do you proceed?, a brain storm?" I suggest trying to anticipate the next move.

"Please, no!", he laughs, "now we proceed systematically."

He sips his water and comes back to the board.

"We will use this example to illustrate the process and then we can see if we want to continue with your real problems."

"Fine with me."

"Now we need to understand why we claim that there is a necessity relationship between the elements with arrows. For example, we can ask why do we think that to be at peace with yourself is necessary to protect our friendship?"

"This is obvious. I prefer to stay troubled before hurting a friend. After all, this is only a job."

"Well, thanks for that. What you said is close to an assumption. Let me rephrase it for you: 'because our friendship is meaningful for you'."

I laugh and say, "Of course, I can rely only on you to replenish my Jack Daniel's reserve twice a year."

"A to C is similar. To be at peace with yourself you need to have your problems solved because…"

"… Because otherwise my job is in jeopardy".

"Good, those are usually solid and strong relationships, AB and AC. Now let us surface other assumptions."

I think I am getting it. "Let me try BD. To protect our friendship I need not to ask you for help because you would take any criticism to your work as an offence."

"Very good! But you see that there is no reason to criticize my work", he laughs. "Seriously, yes, this is the reason I thought, too. And CD'?"

"To have my problems solved I need to ask you for help because… I'm desperate!" We both burst out laughing.

"I would better say, because perhaps TOC could help and there is no risk in trying for a while," Bill says.

"Right, what now?"

"If you can invalidate somehow any of the assumptions, then the arrow is broken and the conflict disappears, evaporates, it is eliminated," he says as he mimics a magical pass with his hands.

"Well, it's a matter of time to invalidate CD', right?" I'm relaxed and finally can see how this could work.

"I prefer to offer you the assurance that you can stop all this work at any time and I will not be offended, fair enough?"

"Perfect, I see now how this really does away with my main concern of hurting our relationship. Are you sure, of what you just offered? Let's get a couple of cappuccinos and we can start with the real stuff." I feel energized.

IX

I want to start with a frequent, irritating yet not the most important issue. If Bill can show me how to solve it, I will feel much better about devoting more time to these logical exercises.

"Bill, before we go to the business problems I want to discuss something that perhaps you consider even irrelevant. I can't understand why very often people come to me with very easy problems. Why don't they solve them instead of distracting me?"

"Richard, this is not irrelevant at all, it is one of those things that Goldratt called 'engines of disharmony'."

"Please, don't start with jargon", I tease him half seriously.

"Right, it is better if you give me an example and we can take it from there."

"That's easy. Yesterday I had to call one big client to inform him that we will change one of the materials in his order, something that doesn't mean worse quality, on the contrary. The case is that we are short of the material for that order, it will take two weeks to resupply and we can substitute it with a better alternative that we have in house. I am willing to increase a little the cost, without increasing the price, to ensure we are on time with the order. The client was very pleased, by the way."

"Okay, the first thing to do is to verbalize the fact that irritates or bothers you. There are some rules: it is a full sentence in present tense, describing a fact, without any explanation, and without blaming."

"Well, the commercial manager doesn't have a good process to deal with these issues. I am tired of telling him to put a process, but things like this keep coming to me when he is not available."

"So he was not available and someone from production wanted to start an order but needed permission to substitute the material."

"Exactly, I don't know why they can't solve it without me."

"First, we need the fact that bothers you."

"I already told you. The commercial manager doesn't have the right process to deal with contingencies."

"Well, Richard, I am here to help you with the process. First, you are pointing your finger to someone else, blaming. Second, what you claim it is not the problem, it's the lack of a solution that you have in mind. You should think more about the fact that bothers you, not what you think is the solution. Try again."

Second thoughts! Second thoughts! Maybe this was not a good idea after all. "The fact is that I had to use twenty minutes in something that someone else could do. That's a fact, right?"

"Yes, that's a fact. Let us rephrase it in a way that we can use now. What about 'Frequently I must use my time to solve problems that others can solve', does this phrase represent what bothers you about the general issue?"

"Yes, when it is not a material, it is an urgent freight, or a permission to work overtime. I don't like being baby sitter of people around here."

"Okay, the first step in the process is done, you stated the fact. In TOC we call that an undesirable effect or UDE, because we believe it is not an inevitable fact of life but the symptom of something deeper, the cause. And the cause for an UDE is always a conflict, like the cloud that we used before. Now we need to build the cloud to define clearly the conflict that causes this fact to become real for you and give you the ulcer we are treating, right?"

"So we draw five boxes with arrows and we write in them, that's all?"

"It sounds easy, but simple is seldom easy. The next step is to answer this question: what is damaged by the fact? In other words, what bothers you is that you need something that you can't have because of this fact."

"Isn't it obvious? I need that my time is not wasted."

Bill goes to the board and writes:

B
My time is not wasted

"Good enough. The second step is to answer the question: what action would satisfy that need? What is it that you'd want to do to avoid those interruptions?"

"I told you; that the commercial manager had a process."

"You can't take that action, can you? What can _you_ do?"

"Maybe I could tell the guy in production to wait to the commercial manager."

"In other words, denying the help, let others solve it."

"Right, but I can't."

Bill writes on the board:

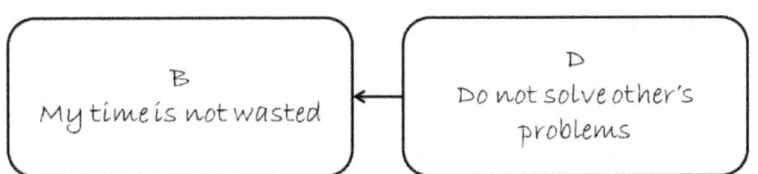

"That leads us to the next step, answering the question: what else is damaged if we take this action permanently?"

"I can't because we are here to give good service, otherwise we will lose market share and eventually go bankrupt."

Bill writes:

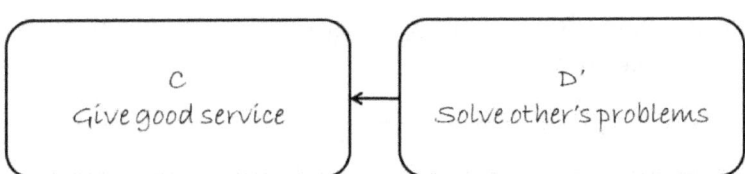

"Note that I added D' immediately because in this case it was obvious that you intervene to give good service. The last step is to understand what objective you cannot achieve if either one of the needs B or C is not satisfied. In other words, why is so important for you to satisfy them?"

I look at the needs as Bill calls them; it is obvious that good service is necessary to have sales and growth in the company. Not wasting my time makes me think of the role of management. Isn't it to make decisions? Maybe I am not wasting my time when I solve problems.

"Richard, come on. What is it that you can't achieve if you don't satisfy both needs at the same time? I see you are in deep thought. Talk to me."

"I am wondering whether it is a waste of my time when I solve problems."

"Good question, right? I have another one related to that one. If you can solve everything, why do you need more managers?"

"You are right. I need time to manage the company, not every single detail. That's why we need an organization, one person cannot do everything. Okay, now it's clear. The objective is to have a prosperous company, this encompasses both the current operation and the future growth. For that I need the time to plan and execute well thought out plans without neglecting the current operation."

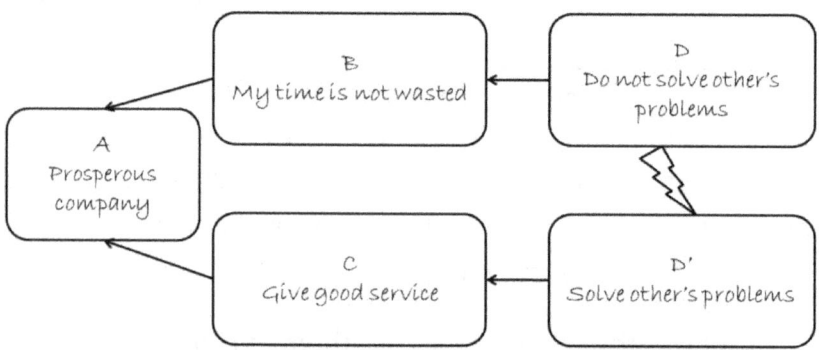

"I like your definition", says Bill as he finishes the cloud. "Now we must read it aloud to see if it makes sense to you. Remember how we did earlier?"

I can barely remember, "On the one hand I don't want to solve other's problems because –".

"Wait", Bill interrupts me, "it is important to read it correctly to see at what extent this is obvious to you or not. Remember to read from left to right and showing clearly the necessity relationship that the arrows indicate. To have A it is necessary to B, and so on. Try it."

I feel I am back in primary school but Bill is the expert, I will play his game. "On the one hand, to have a prosperous company it is necessary that my time is not wasted. To have my time not wasted it is necessary that I don't solve other's problems." It looks logical.

"In the other hand, to have a prosperous company it is necessary to give good service. To give good service it is necessary to solve other's problems." I am starting to have that annoying feeling of being interrupted with emergencies because someone else's job is not done.

"Does it make sense to you?" Bill is staring at me as if reading my mind.

"Well, it does but now I can't help but think that someone is not doing his job."

"Remember what I told you about blaming? Whenever you feel compelled to blame, think again. Why do you think these people come to you with their problems? Because they enjoy bothering you? Better yet, to show how incompetent they are." I know how Bill likes to be sarcastic when he wants to make a point. I smile politely.

"I hope none of the above. But why then?"

"Richard, don't you see that nobody likes coming to you with problems knowing how busy you are? The only reason to do that is that they are accountable for the job and they want it done. That is the opposite of incompetence; at least they show high level of responsibility. So think again, and for that I will show you the next step in the analysis."

Now I am confused. I thought that I had a very good understanding of what was going on and what the solution was. Now it is not so clear and Bill has a point; I can't say that any of our people are incompetent or negligent.

"After building the cloud and defining the problem, the next step is to surface the assumptions and see how to invalidate any of them."

"Wait, wait, you go too fast. How does this cloud define the problem?" I need more clarity.

"What defines a problem? I say that a problem exists when there are facts in reality that are undesirable and they are hard to eliminate. These two characteristics, undesirability and difficulty to eliminate, defines a problem. Do you agree?"

I think for a moment, it is so simple. "So if I can easily solve it, it is not a real problem; okay, I like it. That 's exactly what I don't like about this particular cloud; why things that I can solve easily, are not by the responsible managers."

"Don't jump to conclusions yet. I want to stress that this is not a way to define a problem, it is the only way. And the cloud is the tool to define it. You saw the process, it is simple yet not easy."

"Don't overreact; I think it is easy now." Bill laughs and say, "Okay, Mr. Cloudbuster, let's see what you can do with the next. Now I want to move onto the assumptions."

"The assumptions are those elements that support the logic of our claims. For example, when you say that it is necessary that your time is not wasted to have a prosperous company, you assumed something. Can you tell me?"

"I told you. I can't do everything in the company and I need a team. On top of the regular operations, someone needs to think about the future. The area managers and I are supposed to do that. I can't do it, or they, if we are interrupted with all small things so often."

"What you've just said is profound. Let me elaborate a little bit." Bill grabs a bottle of water from my fridge and takes a drink before speaking.

"TOC or theory of constraints is about simplicity as you already are experiencing. TOC says that every system has a goal, and it cannot deliver more units of its goal than the most constrained element. It is like a chain that cannot resist more than what its weakest link can."

This is common place, but Bill seems to be saying something important. I keep quiet.

"A company is a particular type of system, it is an organization whose goal is to make money, along with two other conditions: satisfying both the employees and the market."

"Wait, before you object let me explain a little bit more. You need the market buying your stuff to make money, and for that you need the collaboration of the employees. Here I even include the suppliers, to enable you to have your materials to produce, and the environment to be sustainable."

"It makes sense", I say, this is not new anymore. It is more and more frequent to hear the same discourse about the social responsibility of the companies. Bill put it in a simpler way and I like it better, because it shows that this so called social responsibility is nothing but a condition to do good business in the long term, not the supposed charity that some seem to understand and preach.

"Then, as any system, a company has a constraint that prevents it to make more units of its intended goal."

"You mean limited capacity or not enough market share?", I'm interested now.

"Yes, those are temporary bottlenecks for the life of the company. With enough cash you can expand on those. But after many years developing TOC, Goldratt came to the conclusion that the ultimate constraint of any organization is management attention". Bill drinks more water and I can reflect on what he's just said.

"You claim that having more management attention this company would make more profits?"

"The amount of management attention is limited. What I say is that as long as the management attention is wasted, the company cannot prosper."

I feel a sting in the stomach. It is not only me, it is all the team that waste time day in and day out. And this is so painfully obvious! I always knew that if only I could devote more time to the important strategic issues, the company would do much better. Damn it! I am not concerned about spending this time with Bill or on these subjects any more.

"So what you are saying is that this apparently small matter of solving other's problems is killing the company!" I can't believe this realization.

"Don't be so dramatic, Richard, your company is doing well. I guess that you are not happy yourself but the market recognizes good value and the shareholders have no complaints."

"That's true, but at what cost! All my team works long hours and we don't make the difference, not a significant one, we are back on the grind stone every quarter with the same issues."

"Okay, enough crying baby", says Bill with a smile, "the assumption for AB is solid. Let us look into the arrow that bothers you the most."

"After this last five minutes I hate being forced to solve all those problems, wasting my precious time."

"Okay, let us ask ourselves, why do we claim is necessary to solve other's problems to give good service?"

"That's easy; because they can't solve them by themselves."

Bill writes on the board:

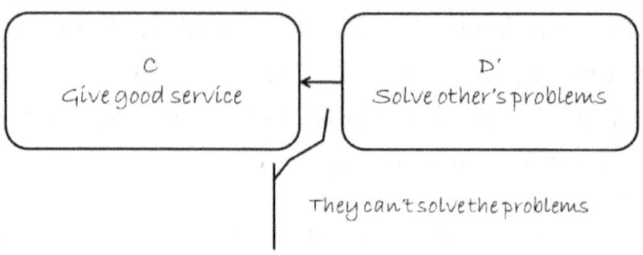

They can't solve the problems

"We need more clarity, Richard. You mean they don't know how to solve them?"

"Very unlikely, it is a simple matter, they know what to do, but they can't because in these exceptions they need to talk to clients and the people in production don't have authorization to call clients. You understand the chaos if we let anyone call the clients for any little thing."

"I see, may I rephrase it?" Bill is very cautious with the words.

"In my opinion, the assumption is 'there is a misalignment between responsibility and authority'. That explains not only this case, but most likely any other case where managers are approached by subordinates to solve issues for which the subordinates are accountable for but they can't take the appropriate actions. Does it make sense?"

Damn! Again this is so simple and clear. Where is the catch? "Well, I see what you are saying, but you surely agree that authority must have limits."

"Of course I agree. Do you agree that while this misalignment exists you will receive all this extra work?"

"Now that I think of it, my area managers, especially the commercial manager, are the ones who receive most of the interruptions. No wonder they are reluctant to discuss strategic ideas. The reality is that they don't have time."

"Then it would be a good thing for all of you if you can fix all the misalignments, correct?"

"Yes, but they are too many and too different."

"Yes, Richard, but all of them have in common the element of misalignment, which can be described as a cloud."

"So, we could use the cloud to detect the misalignment every time and look how to invalidate the assumption?" I think that I understand.

"Exactly. Usually the assumption in these cases of misalignment of authority and responsibility is a policy of the company. You can use this procedure to detect what part of what policy should be changed." After a pause, Bill continues, "You just told me, we can not let everyone call the clients for any little thing, this is a policy."

"I knew it was a process that we lack!", I say with a grin.

"Richard, my friend, it is always a lack of process. The problem is that many times procedures are designed in such a way that the medicine is worse than the disease. This one is simple and effective. You should practice it and then teach it to your managers, so all of you can change all the policies that are constraining the company. I will send you the article[1] that Goldratt wrote to explain this procedure. I advise you to keep a copy for future reference."

---

[1] "Empowerment", article written by Dr. Eliyahu Goldratt, http://new.goldratt.com/empower.htm,

"Policies are constraints?" Bill is now confusing me a little bit.

"In our experience of many years and thousands of companies, there are on average seven misalignments per level. Policies are there for a good reason from the past. Inertia causes that policies are not updated and they can block the organization, constraining it, creating a source of disharmony, wasting your and your management valuable time and attention."

"It makes sense. We internally have discussed such cases that are grotesque, but nobody took the time to systematically revise them."

"Have you seen how many urgent things that interrupt you come from these misalignments?"

"Sure, it is not the cause for most of them, but it is significant. Eliminating the cause will definitely release a good deal of my time."

"This is one of the ways that TOC eliminates the causes for the urgent."

"Now I see what you meant with that mail of yours. But there are many other urgent things that don't stem from this cause. Do you have more tricks in your hat?" I am gaining momentum with the hope that such magical promise could be true.

"Sure, however this is enough for today. I propose that we meet again to discuss another source for the urgent and how to eliminate it. For that, I need you doing homework. Remember the song? Relax, I need some information first; just the basic facts, can you show me where it hurts?"

Who can forget Pink Floyd. "I hope that we will not become comfortably dumb at the end."

"Why, do you feel uncomfortable now?," says Bill with a laugh. "What I need is a list of undesirable effects, UDEs, from different areas of the company."

"Okay, when can you do the next session?"

"How about next Thursday? We need at least three hours."

"Three hours!, I can't make it that day, but Friday afternoon it is good for me and we can end it with beers."

"You know how to sell it, man. Done, see you next Friday."

X

This week I practiced what we discussed in our last session with Bill. Following the instructions in the article and a couple of tips over Skype that Bill gave me, I already successfully changed two policies. It was so obvious in hindsight that it feels embarrassing. I hope to start enjoying the effects soon.

This Friday started with more problems than usual. I am tempted to postpone our meeting with Bill to work on the most pressing problems. He should be here in one hour. I ask for a salad and a soda and start a list of the problems, trying to write them as UDEs.

The lunch was light and the list short. I thought it would be longer. When I had written all the most pressing issues, and the list had only three problems, I just finished it with all the things that I am worried about nowadays. It is still short, with only twelve items.

The experience of the last meeting showed me that the process may take time so I don't expect to discuss more than the first three this afternoon, but it is good to have the rest just in case.

The phone rings exactly two minutes before our meeting. "Who? Yes, send him in, please."

"Hi Richard, are you ready for some thinking to end the week?"

"Sure, and I already did my homework putting together a list of UDEs," I say as I hand him my list.

"Fantastic!, we will have good material to work on then."

"As you can see I wrote twelve UDEs, but the first three are the most important for me now. I know that we can't address all of them today. I have learned something from you; so we go systematically solving one by one, right?"

"Richard, I like how you put it. We will do all the work systematically. However I think that you will have a nice surprise."

"What do you mean? Do you have a trick to do the work faster?" If it is possible, Bill is right; I'd be delighted.

"It is not faster, Richard, but it could be shorter than you think."

I wait while Bill explains this riddle; shorter but not faster. Frankly, I don't care which one as long as we can solve everything fast.

"Look, one of the pillars of TOC is the belief in the inherent simplicity that lies at the bottom of any organization. This means that all of your UDEs, your undesirable effects, are just that, effects stemming from only one root cause."

"So you are saying that these twelve problems are effects of only one cause? And finding that cause and solving it, all of them are solved?" It is hard to believe. Everybody is talking about different solutions for problems in different areas. For example, in logistics there are solutions for better forecasts and also better systems to manage warehouses and more sophisticated algorithms to calculate routes for the trucks. In sales I have seen many techniques to handle objections, or make a sale through questions that reveal the needs. In marketing there are many different approaches. And production, a world by itself with all the continuous improvement techniques, quality assurance, TPM, lean. How come Bill is saying that he can find only one cause for all my problems in the company? Can it be what he meant with the 'unified field theory of management'?

"Richard, where are you my friend?"

"I was thinking."

"What were you 'sinking' about?", he says with a smile, but I can guess that he knows.

"Are you serious about this claim of finding only one root cause for all the twelve problems of my list? They are from very different areas of the company. I thought that dividing it in small chunks, the whole pie would be much easier to eat."

"Tell me something, have you had the experience of taking an action in one area that affected others?"

"Yes, I don't say they are completely independent. I just said that –." Bill raises his hand and I wait.

"Richard, please, bear with me for a minute. All the areas of your company are parts of the same whole. I would say that the surprise should be if the actions in one area didn't impact another."

"Yes, but we need to divide the organization in order to manage it. This is obvious, otherwise it would be too complex. And besides, how would I hold accountable each of the managers if there are no frontiers?"

"But you agree that all of them are parts of the same whole, don't you?"

"Yes." I don't see the practical use of this and we are using valuable time.

"Therefore, you also agree that you want to manage the whole and not each part."

"Yes." My patience is reaching its limit with all these trivialities.

"Then, the only prudent way to manage a company is with a holistic approach. Holistic comes from holism, the philosophy that says that the universe is correctly seen in terms of interacting wholes that are more than the mere sum of elementary particles."

"I'd like to have a deep philosophical conversation with you, but we have work to do now." It's my turn to focus my friend.

"You are right. That is what I want to do as well. I want to show you how taking only the first three UDEs in your list we can find the root conflict. Remember, the cause for an UDE is always an underlying conflict."

"Okay, I'm with you. Let's start with the first UDE. 'I need to increase sales by at least 10% in one month'."

"Richard, we need to rephrase that UDE into a fact that wouldn't presume your desired solution."

Bill is implacable, but he knows. "Well, the fact is that we don't have enough sales volume."

"It wasn't that hard," he says as he writes it on the board.

Now let us build the cloud. After three minutes we have it.

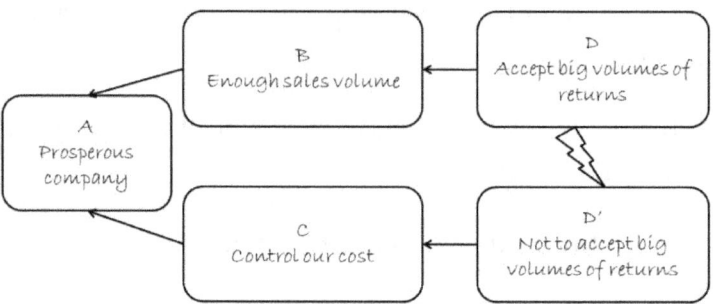

"It looks obvious to me", I say, "Should we go to the assumptions now?"

"Nope. We are doing a full analysis now, so we first need to understand the full problem first. What's the second UDE?"

I look at my list and read, knowing that something will be corrected, "We have too much inventories of finished goods."

Surprisingly Bill writes it on the board without any comment. "Can you build the cloud? You said it is easy, didn't you?"

It takes more than three minutes this time, with Bill helping me to distinguish between needs and actions. It was not so easy but I think I got it.

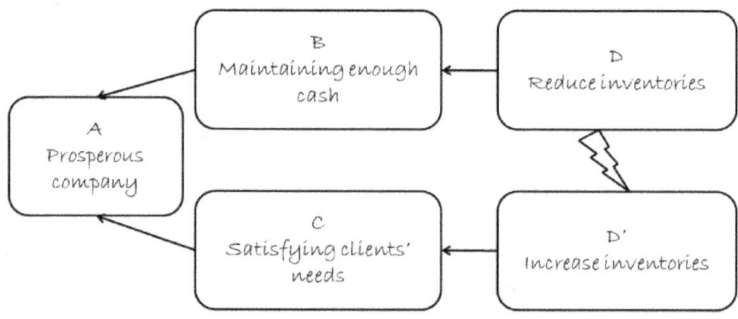

"Can you see the similarities?", asks Bill. Of course I can, but I never doubted that there was a relationship. The problem is that I can't do much with that. I nod and wait.

"And the third?" Bill is running.

"Our production cost is too high."

"Richard, I need more clarity about this one. Do you mean that you are spending more money now than in the past to make the products your plant is producing?"

"Not quite, we even have reduced some expenses. The problem is that our production costs are too high, and our margins are shrinking, no mention about the competitiveness."

"I see, we can work with this for now, but definitely we will revisit how your company calculates things later on. Can you build the cloud alone?"

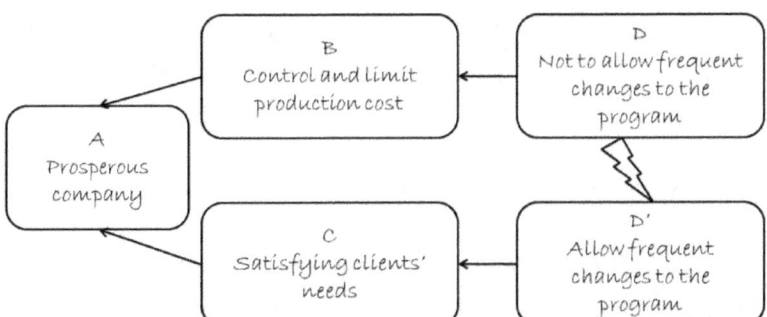

"These are my most pressing priorities, because I need the cash that is tied up to the inventories. I know that the best way to get that cash is increasing sales without giving the discounts, and I don't want to compromise on our competitiveness in cost." Explained in this way it is clear that all the three are related to each other. But I can't see how only one cause is responsible for the three.

"What about similarities now, do you see a clear pattern?"

"I can see similar things like the objective, which is the same for the three. And there are similarities in the needs as well."

"Let us write the elements in separate lists and try to extract the essential concept underlying to each one." Bill goes to the board and makes a table with five columns, with the letters A, B, C, D and D' in the first row.

"The first one is obvious. The generic A is 'Prosperous company'." And he writes it in the last row.

"To do the same with the rest we must first see whether a flip exists." As I look confused, Bill continues. "A flip happens when one cloud has one of the corresponding entities on a side that is in the opposite location in one of the other clouds. It is all about intuition to realize this, but the reason for it to happen is that the point of view of the person building the cloud can be more biased to protect more one need than the other."

"I understand better with an example. Do you see a flip here?" I stop Bill before he lectures me too much about theory.

"You tell me. Look at the C element in the first cloud and the B in the third."

I read them: 'Control our cost' and 'Control and limit production cost'. Both are almost the same. I see what Bill is saying. "So we take one cloud and we flip it, swapping B with C, and of course D with D'".

"Of course," Bill smiles at me. "So we can write down all the B's, all the C's and so on."

I look at the board and read the B's:

- Control our cost
- Control and limit production cost
- Maintaining enough cash

"What do you think the essence of all those three is?" Bill waits while I think.

"It is something related to the cost, to the limited resources that we have."

"Would you say these are concerns related to the external environment or the internal?" I can see Bill has something in mind. Why is he playing this riddle game instead of just saying it?

"All of those are internal concerns or needs, as you call them. We could say the essence is 'good use of our resources'".

"That is good. I believe that you can formulate it in more practical terms. Think why you would care about using well your resources."

"Why don't you tell me what you think?", I don't like being manipulated.

"Richard, it is important that you use your own words. I have seen this cloud so many times that, unless your company is an exception among hundreds, there is no surprise. But please think a little bit more why you think it is important to give good use to your resources. It is not for the sake of showing how good you are at using them, right?"

"Of course not. It is because otherwise we couldn't operate for long, could we?"

"Fine, don't be irritated. You got it." Bill goes to the board and writes in the last row of the B's: 'Protect the current operation'. "Do you agree that this need represents the essence of all the similar needs?"

"Yes, I like it." Now I see what Bill said. I will try the generic C. Bill seems to have noticed it and waits silently.

"The three C's are related with good service and more sales. I would say that even it is an internal concern, the essence is connected with a growing participation in our markets."

"Very well put. How would you formulate it?" Bill is ready to write.

"I'd say that the essence in this case is 'Ensure future growth', that requires more sales and good service."

"As you could see, this is not a triviality and requires some profound thinking. However A, B and C are the easiest ones. Let us try deducing the generic D now."

I look at the board:

- Not to accept big volumes of returns
- Reduce inventories
- Not to allow frequent changes to the programs

"Not easy at all. When I look at them I can hear my finance manager." This is the first laugh that we have in a long while.

"You are on the money, come on!" I can't decide whether Bill is excited or impatient.

"What do you think of 'Take actions to reduce expenses or investments' as the essence for D?"

"I agree. Perfect. Now D' is the opposite." Bill goes to the board and builds the cloud, writing 'Generic cloud' above it.

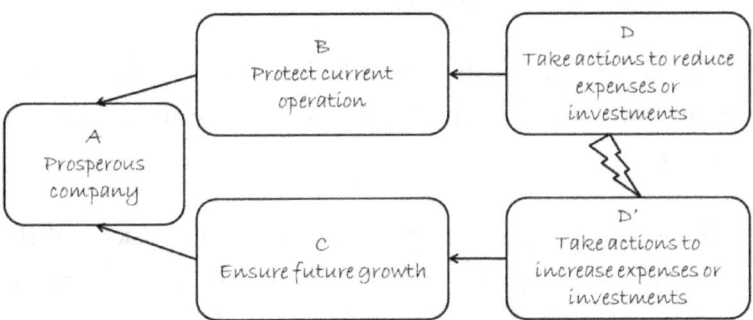

"Richard, please, read it aloud to see whether it makes sense to you."

I have done this several times now so I'm confident to do it right. "On the one hand, to have a prosperous company we need to protect the current operation. To protect the current operation we need to take actions to reduce expenses or investments." So far, so good I think.

"On the other hand, to have a prosperous company we need to ensure future growth. To ensure future growth we need to take actions to increase expenses or investments."

We stay in silent for some seconds. "Is this always the same? I mean, you've done this before. In all the cases did you get this same one?"

"Yes and no. It is always the same essence, but the words change." Bill is visibly satisfied with the result.

"Richard, you had nine other UDEs in your list. Can you see how all of them stem from this same conflict?"

I thought we were over, but Bill is right. The claim was that we'd find a root cause for everything. I look at my list and take one of the other nine randomly.

"Let's see, I have here something that looks completely unrelated. Sometimes we don't have enough room in our warehouses."

Bill writes this one down on a post-it and sticks it at the top of the board, and just above the cloud, he writes D and D', side by side, but adding to each one the words 'There is pressure to'.

"Can you tell me why you get to that situation?", Bill asks.

"Because we produce more stock than what we sell in a period, and it accumulates."

"And why is that?", Bill smiles at me.

"Okay, I see the connection. The pressure to increase inventories leads to this directly." This is powerful.

"Yes, and we can easily tie it up to the conflict with logic of cause and effect, as I did here."

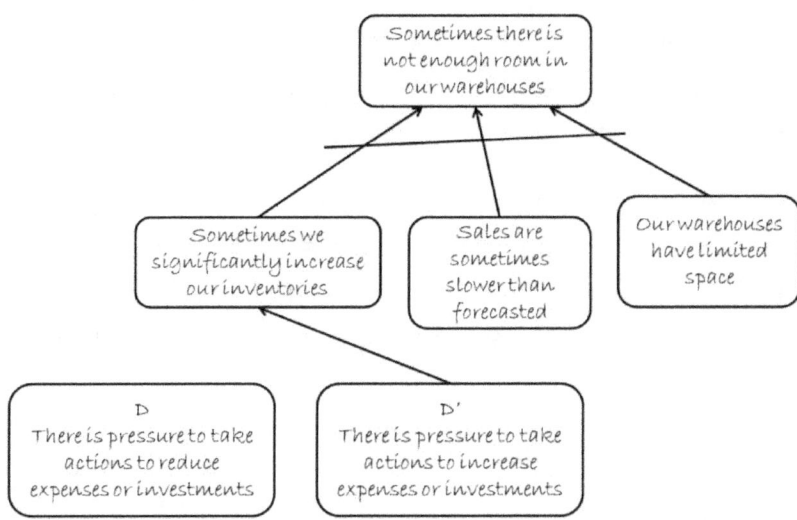

"This is read showing the logic," Bill says, "from bottom up, where the tail of an arrow starts from a cause and the tip of the arrow arrives to an effect. In this case, these relationships are read like this," and pointing to each of the elements he starts reading.

"If there is pressure to take actions to increase investments, then sometimes we significantly increase the inventories. Here we could have another assumption to explain that inventories are a type of investment, but it is so obvious that we can omit it."

"So we don't need to include everything, only the elements that could be not so obvious." I start seeing how this is practical.

"Yes, my advice is to include all that you have doubts about. Now, see that we have three arrows that are connected indicating an 'AND' connector."

"So more than one arrow without the connector indicates 'OR', it is either cause. But with 'AND' you need all of them to have the effect, correct?"

"Perfect, you got it. So now we have the following: if sometimes we significantly increase the inventories and sometimes sales are slower than forecasted and our warehouses have limited space, then sometimes there is not enough room in our warehouses."

"It sounds obvious."

"Thanks, that's the best compliment for a good logical construction. Can you give me another UDE that you don't see clearly the connection to the conflict?"

"Looking at my list, the other eight are all related either with plans of growth or with protecting the current operation. Fine, you won this one." I say smiling at Bill but with uncertainty about the real use of this understanding yet.

"I think that we deserve a couple of cappuccinos now."

"Good idea. While they bring them, let me watch my emails and reply the most urgent ones. It is just twenty minutes."

"Perfect. Do you have a newspaper?" I hand him today's paper and I see that Bill goes directly to solve the puzzles. It's fun to be a consultant!

XI

"We still have time today, so I propose that we finish the analysis looking for a suitable solution for this core conflict in your specific case." Bill is all business when he is not playing in his smart phone or solving puzzles.

"Do you think we can get there today? Amazing!" Not that I'm not happy with that, it is just that only one afternoon to have all this work done sounds incredible. I always heard from strategic consultants that it takes weeks to do a proper diagnosis and to decide a prudent action plan.

"Why? Don't you see that once we have found the inherent simplicity in the system it is all about details? Anyway, today we are not going to lay out all the details, but we can set the strategic direction."

"So tell me if I'm wrong. The next step is to surface an assumption that we could invalidate somehow." I like this, when the process is simple, I can work comfortably.

"Well said, you go fast. What is the side of the conflict that bothers you the most?"

So this is one of the recipes, looking at what side bothers you the most. Interesting approach, and my intuition is good at it.

"I can answer that very fast. It is the part that forces us to cut costs to protect the current operation. It is like if this company was founded to save money instead of generating it!"

"I see that I'm not the only sarcastic one here." Bill says smiling. "To protect the current operation we need to take actions to reduce expenses and investments because..."

"Because cash is the most important resource to keep the operation running."

"Agree, and I don't see how to invalidate this one."

It was not that simple after all. I will try the other one.

"To ensure the future growth we need to increase expenses or investments. Well I wouldn't have any problem with that provided the cash comes from the current operation."

"That is good. Go on, what is the assumption?" Bill goes to the board and he is ready to write.

"The assumption is that we can't generate continually cash at a higher rate than we consume it."

"Yes, I agree. So the action in D' actually says that you need to provide cash before you get the return, under the assumption that the return is secured. How frequently do you have to put cash on a project that didn't return what was expected?"

"Don't remind me. The last experience was the marketing plan. We spent a significant amount of cash and the returns were slim compared with the projections. And after the fact, there are many explanations, except that the plan was high risk in the first place, and the unintended consequences made it worse."

"So you say that you need actions that produce a net positive cash flow, with a low risk."

"I didn't need part of the day to get to this conclusion, I knew all the time!", Arrgghhh!!! I'm again fearing more trivialities.

"Richard, this is important, because you are setting the necessary conditions to tell when a tactic is good or bad." Bill writes on the board 'Conditions for a good tactic', underlines it and writes just below: 'Throughput must grow faster than operating expenses', and 'Not taking real risks.'

"What is throughput? Is it production?"

"Not exactly. In TOC, throughput is defined as the rate of generating units of the goal through sales. In the case of a company, the units of the goal are measured in money."

"Is it the gross margin then?" Why to put different names to already known concepts.

"You could say that, yes. But we don't want to confuse things and the best way to formulate it is the sales price minus the raw material. This will be a very good approximation in the vast majority of the cases."

"Okay. And why did you write 'real risks'? Are there of any other kind? My problems are not from lala land..."

"Oh, yes! There are presumed risks just because there was not enough thinking in the first place. Considering false risks is almost as damaging as not considering the real ones. There is always a quota of risk in all we do, but we will see how we can reduce most of the perceived risks and take care only of the real ones."

"Well, those two conditions sound so obvious that I don't see the need for more."

"Really? What if you run out of capacity of any type?" Bill is being paranoid now.

"Okay, I see, the other condition is not to exhaust any resource." As I say it, Bill writes the third condition.

"So, we have the three conditions for the action that would invalidate the assumption under CD', which was that the expenditure of cash to grow is usually taking high risks."

"It sounds promising. What is that action? Come on, you told me this was a generic cloud, so this action must be generic, too." I am eager to hear what brilliant idea Bill will produce from his magical hat now.

"Very well, that is true. I will give it to you and we discuss it a little bit before you dismiss it as another triviality, okay?"

"I can't promise you anything," I tease him, "but go ahead, make my day."

"The generic tactic is to build a decisive competitive edge, and the capabilities to capitalize on it, in big enough markets, without exhausting the company's resources and without taking real risks."

"And you said that without a blink? What a mouthful!", we both laugh.

"Seriously, Bill, what is the practicality of such phrase? Isn't it the same as all the strategic marketing theories are saying about differentiation? I don't want to be rude, but this is obvious. What am I actually learning from this?"

"I suppose it is the same. Is it incorrect?" Bill looks calm, and very serious, too.

"Incorrect? I didn't say that, it is just so obvious. Have you read that book about blue oceans?"

"You mean 'Blue Ocean Strategy' by Chan Kim and Reneé Mauborgne? Yes, I did."

As Bill names it I can find it on my shelf. I take it and read the cover aloud: "How to create uncontested market space and make the competition irrelevant. I read it last year. It is a very good book, with out of the box ideas."

"And what do you think about the concept? Don't you think that if you had a blue ocean this conflict vanishes, evaporates?"

"Of course, but it is not so simple to have brilliant ideas like those, my friend. The biggest issue these guys report is that many tried and failed, before it really worked. I do not want to die trying if you get my drift."

Bill looks thoughtful for a while and finally say, "Richard, it is not easy but it is simple, and this is the key. A simple and elegant solution is the hardest to find, and to imitate. In hindsight everyone says it was obvious, but before that, the idea is hidden to everybody."

"I read the book and I saw that many of the ideas presented to create blue oceans were not new; many tried them before. The authors tell you that many companies went bankrupt before the successful ones could tell the nice story. I don't want to try different things just to teach someone else."

"True, but I want you to consider the concept for a minute. If you could think of an idea that creates a blue ocean for your company, in big enough markets and you also can build the capabilities to capitalize on it, isn't that by itself something that breaks the conflict? And don't forget the part of not taking real risks or exhausting the resources."

I don't know whether we are back to fantasyland or this is going somewhere. We still have a couple of hours before the beers and we could do some real work instead of this exercise.

"Bill, if we could do that, of course the conflict is broken. We can grow the business with much more certainty. Is there any practical idea for us today?" I want him to acknowledge the fact that we are using my most scarce resource, my management attention.

"Bear with me for a couple of minutes and focus on the following. Can you think of another tactic that can break the conflict? I mean, in general terms as this one. Take your time."

I think hard and say, "There is no other idea in front of me now, so even if it were another one, I can't think of it just now."

"You have plenty of time from now on to try and find a better way. Let me tell you our experience in TOC. This is not only a way to break the generic conflict. We believe that it is the only way to do it."

"Okay, I will take your word for it. What now?"

"Please, consider carefully the consequences of what I've just told you. This means that unless you eliminate the conflict, you will be condemned to fight the consequences, the undesirable effects, forever. And you will be caught in the vicious cycle that you don't like, until you can eliminate the root cause. Even worse, all these consequences erode the human relationships, in your company and with suppliers and clients."

"Who is dramatic now? I am not alone in this situation. I know many managers that have similar problems. Do you mean all of them are caught in the same trap? How come that nobody has already said it aloud? Because I must tell you that you are the first in telling such things that I've heard of. What about universities and their business management education?" I feel much more uncomfortable with this realization because it makes so much sense, and I am trying to drown its power with words. I don't see how I could possibly think of such a gorgeous idea today.

"Richard, remember what I told you that evening about judging the value of something based on the majority's opinion? And you just showed me a book that tells exactly this. Furthermore, let me tell you that there are hundreds of MBA's that include 'The Goal' in their syllabus for some years now. However, a significant change in the academia takes generations. I don't know why. And I don't want to use your time here discussing that."

"Exactly, I want to do something practical." I am relieved that Bill is on the same page.

"So, what is your verdict? Do you see that a blue ocean along with the low risk, the capabilities to capitalize on it and not exhausting resources is the only way out for your problem?"

"I must painfully say yes. And I say painfully because we have been working hard with my management around this concept when I read that book. We haven't been passively suffering our problems, you know? Even we tried things, like using our new forecasting system for our clients, but they wouldn't listen. There is so much polite distrust between us and them that the best idea won't work."

"So you already reduced the expectations of what it's possible because of that." I try to protest but Bill continues. "This is one of the worst consequences of accepting conflicts as a given; people stop thinking just because they had failures in their attempts of breaking the conflict."

"I haven't stopped thinking!" Now I am a CEO that doesn't think!, Bill is close to the edge.

"Calm down, I only say that my belief is that there is always a way to break any conflict. In this case I also say that the only way to break this particular conflict is to build such incredible thing as I told you before. It is not easy; and it is worthwhile. Would you like to know how to systematically find your blue ocean? We can do it now. And you also will see that it is simple."

"You already have it, don't you? Are you a sadist?", I say laughing.

"What did a masochist say to a sadist? – Make me suffer. And what was the sadist's reply? – I don't want to." Even though the joke is very old, I laugh anyway and I get ready for the next step. This is exciting.

"What about a break with cappuccinos and we end the day with the analysis of your market?" Bill is not that sadist after all, but I am afraid that we are not prepared for this analysis.

"What? I didn't ask for any statistics of consumption or data about all the distributors. Besides, the marketing manager is out of the office today. Shouldn't we wait for him?"

"We don't need data or more people now. You know everything that we need to know. Please, ask for the cappuccinos, reply to your urgent emails and get ready to work in ten minutes."

"Yes, sir!" I admit that Bill looks very confident and I feel energized with the idea of finding a blue ocean for us.

XII

Bill erases the board and starts. "We are going to do the same thing that we did with your own undesirables effects, but this time we need your clients' undesirable effects."

"That's easy, they complain a lot." Bill smiles at me and waits.

"Okay, the first and more frequent complaint is about prices."

"So you mean they ask for more discounts, right?" As I nod, Bill continues, "This sounds like an UDE of yours. You don't like when they ask for lower prices. Put yourself in their shoes and think what the fact that they don't like is."

"I guess that they want to make more money at our expense."

"I would say that the feeling is mutual," Bill says and waits. He is just waiting.

This exercise of putting me in their shoes is not that easy as I thought. At least I am not apparently fulfilling Bill's standards.

"They want lower prices because they want to make more money. So the fact would be the usual, profits are not high enough."

Bill thinks for a second and says, "I would prefer the term profitability instead of profit. What about saying: profitability is not satisfactory." I nod and he writes it down on the board. I really don't care if we say profits or profitability, so I don't argue.

"What else?", Bill is waiting again, as if he was the one pressed by the time.

I have a fresh one. "They have too much surplus in the shops." Bill writes it silently and turns again waiting.

"They have too many shortages," I say it but I can't help it but thinking of their stubbornness for not accepting our offer to help them with the forecast. Bill writes it down.

"We already have three. How many more do we need?" I thought that the magical number was three.

"Try looking at different aspects of their business and see what other UDEs of theirs you can think of. We need at least two more."

"I know that cash is always tight because they ask us for more credit. The fact is that they are very often tight on cash flow."

"Very good, you are thinking in terms of cause and effect," Bill says as he writes that one down. I feel like I'm back in school with the compliment, but I don't want to interrupt this flow by teasing him now. But he deserves it, though.

"Do you have any other for the last?"

I must think. Wait, I have visited some stores and in the backroom I saw grotesque situations like a 42"-plasma that had its screen broken because there was a big pile of boxes just above it.

"I'm sure that there is scrap in their warehouses, things that they can't sell and must write off," I finally say.

Bill writes on the board 'Sometimes there is significant amount of scrap'.

I look at the list and I can imagine how all those five facts are constant pains in the neck to our clients. And now I also can see there are connections of cause and effect between them. We probably need to do the same as we discussed for my company. I don't see where we are going now. But I learned that Bill is full of nice surprises and I wait.

"Well done, I believe these five are good enough for us to work."

"Can I build the cloud for the first one?" I feel powerful knowing what to do.

"What for? Forget the clouds, we can go directly to connect all these UDEs in a logical tree that will show us a significant need of these clients."

"You are changing the process now, please don't confuse me."

I see it coming, Bill never forgives an opportunity, "Hush, hush, baby, you will soon see that this is not any different. The only thing that we'll do differently now is that instead of finding the core cloud, we'll build the logic just until the point where your company comes in."

"I see, very clever. If we can see where we can trim the UDEs, we can create value to our clients. The deeper in the tree, the better. I like it, how do we go about it?"

"We first take one of the UDEs and try to find an obvious connection with another. Take the first one: 'Profitability is not satisfactory', for example. Do you have a pad of post-its?"

As I hand him the pad he erases the board, writes it down on one square and puts it on the board. As he does it, I write down the other four in respective post-its. I like this way of mind mapping.

"I suppose that the scrap is directly tied up to the profitability." I hand the paper to Bill and he puts it on the board, below the first one, and he draws an arrow from the last one to the first one.

"If there is significant amount of scrap then profitability is not satisfactory," Bill reads aloud. "Can you choose another one to connect to either one?"

I feel something is missing. "Don't we need more to explain the unsatisfactory profitability from this fact?"

"Yes, we do. But we first build the backbone with all our UDEs, and then we complete the logic with all the missing elements."

I like processes! "I believe that if they have too much surplus in the shops, then sometimes there is significant amount of scrap." I stand up and put the UDE below and draw the arrow.

Bill sits and waits. I put the other two and read aloud, "If they have too much surplus in the shops then they are often tight on cash flow. And if they are often tight on cash flow then they have too many shortages, which in turn lead to unsatisfactory profitability."

"Well done. Now we need to introduce all the assumptions that solidify the logic to our tree. For each relationship we can ask why we think that exists. For example, why do you say that tight cash flow leads to shortages?" Bill is comfortably seated now while I work on the board.

"That is because they need the cash to replenish what they are short of." I grab another post-it and add this element, guessing where to put it and connect the arrows to indicate the 'AND'. Bill smiles visibly pleased. "Go on," he says, "you can finish it on your own."

After a while I have filled the board with the following tree:

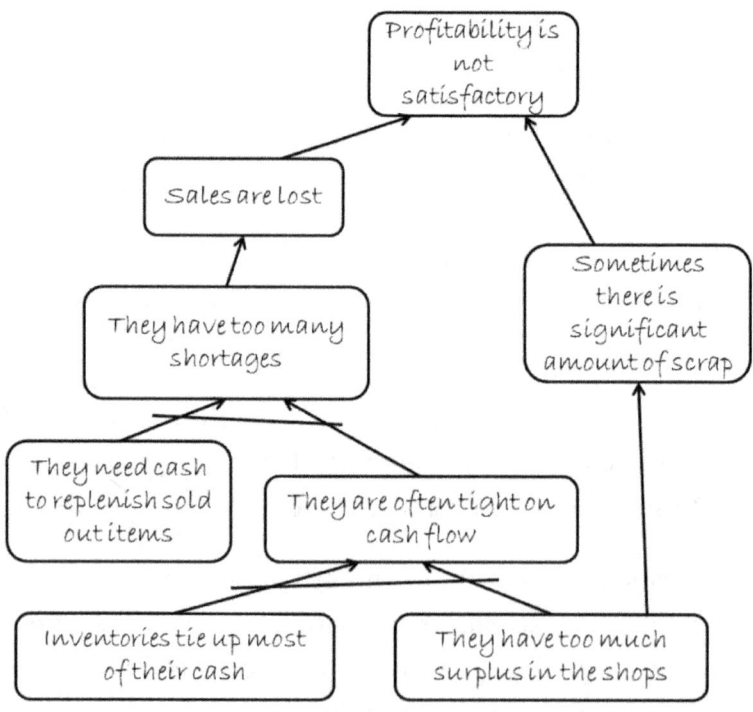

"Not bad," says Bill, "for a start."

"I see how bad the surplus is for them. And I see that one of the causes is that their cash is tied up in inventory. I could offer my goods on consignment, but that had bad results when we offered it in the past. Please tell me that you have a better idea".

"I have a better idea," Bill says. "My idea is that you ask 'why' a couple of times more. You already had the idea of challenging the fact of tying up cash to inventories and you didn't like it. Fine, there is another cause here. For now, we don't know the causes of the surplus, what you've just developed are the consequences. First, do you realize that when your clients lose sales, you lose sales?"

Damn! Again the obvious and how painfully it hits me. If I accept consignment, the surplus is not gone. It is only that the risk would be mine instead. Yes, to dive down a little bit more to understand the causes for the surplus will be worthwhile.

I see that Bill is waiting while I think. "What is the next step then?", I ask, not sure how to proceed from here.

"Ask yourself why there is surplus in a shop."

"They bought too much," I'm hesitant when I state the obvious. Bill writes it down on post-it and adds it below with an arrow.

"That means that you say 'too much' compared to something, right? I'm sure that you are happy when the clients buy a lot, aren't you?" Bill doesn't miss an opportunity to point out the obvious contradictions in our actions. We are the ones pushing the clients to buy too much!

"I see where you are going. You can't blame us for doing our job! The clients should know when to stop."

"Richard, can you tell me how do your clients calculate how much to buy?"

"There are different types of clients; those who have forecasting systems and those who just guess."

Bill laughs and says, "What is the difference?"

"Come on Bill, you know better than that. Statistics can be used to forecast the trends and that information will help a lot knowing what to buy."

"I fully agree. Do you understand that your clients are not doing that? They are trying to forecast the future consumption for each product they buy from you. It is not a trend, they try to anticipate single events. How frequently do they buy the same product?"

"Some of them buy weekly, some daily and some monthly. It depends on their size."

"Sorry if you misunderstood me. Is this frequency for the average product or to place an order?"

"I see, for a single product it varies depending on if it is a fast runner or not."

"Let me ask it differently. Do you think that your clients will replenish in an order all the products that were sold since the last order? Do they do it even if they've sold only one unit?"

"Of course they don't. They wait until their inventories are reduced, otherwise the surplus would be worse, wouldn't it?" I believe that Bill is thinking out of the *bucket* now.

"We are trying to understand that. So it is fair to say that even the biggest clients are placing orders for the same item once a week on average, right? And the smallest ones are doing it once a month or even less frequently?" I nod.

"How long does it take for your company to deliver an order?"

"It depends. If the items are in our stock, in less than two days the goods should be in their warehouse. If we run out of something, most frequently they cancel the order, unless they can wait for the ten days that takes us to produce it."

"And just a final question, what is the amount of inventory that they need to hold for each product?"

"Enough to cover the sales till the next replenishment, right?"

"How would you calculate that? Or they?"

"It is the average sale for the period between replenishments, augmented by a safety factor." I never considered this before, but it is pretty obvious now to look at it in this way.

"In other words, the target for the inventory for each item should be the maximum expected consumption within the replenishment time, factored by the variability of the replenishment time, do you agree?" I ask Bill to repeat it slowly.

"Yes, I agree."

"The replenishment time is the addition of three different times: production lead time, transport lead time and order lead time. This last one is the time between two orders."

"Okay, as we hold inventories, our clients' replenishment time is only transport and order lead times, right?" I like the simple way of analyzing.

"Most of the time, because remember that you have shortages, too."

"Correct, but that's very unlikely."

Bill makes a face but he doesn't say anything and continues. "In your clients' replenishment times, what is the longest component?"

"I already told you that transport is short, one or two days including all the paperwork and picking. So the longest, as you concluded, is order lead time, ranging from one week to more than a month."

"Now, would you agree that the replenishment time is relatively long in most cases?"

"Yes." I start realizing where Bill is going now.

"Knowing that forecast for an item in a shop is very inaccurate, and knowing that forecast deteriorates over time, then for a long replenishment time, the forecast must be quite inaccurate." Bill concludes the cause for the surplus, and I just finish it.

"If the forecast is inaccurate, many times the quantities ordered for some items are more than the required for the sales, leading to surplus. And for other items, the quantities ordered are less than required, leading to early sold outs." This is what I always suspected.

"What are you thinking?", Bill says when I stayed quiet for some seconds.

"I had this idea of offering to our clients the service of using our sophisticated forecasting system to help them with quantities to order. I knew that theirs was much worse and ours would solve the problem. But unfortunately none of them accepted our offer. I guess there is not trust in our relationship. But with this tree we may convince –"

"Stop," Bill says, "don't bother. Don't you see that your system cannot forecast any better at that level of detail?"

"What are you saying? There is no way out?" I'm back to frustration.

"I didn't say that. First, let us put the whole logic together." And he completes some other post-its and puts them on the board.

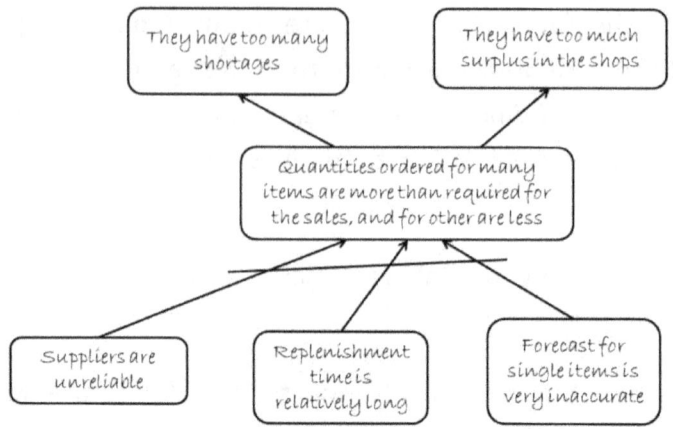

"We are not that unreliable!" I protest.

"You already told me that sometimes you don't have what they ask for. Even if you take this one out, the logic holds." I see the point, but I need more clarity. "If I can take it out, the arrows shouldn't have the connection, right?"

"You can erase that part of the connection, it doesn't make a difference," Bill says, and asks, "Do you see how to change any of these causes?"

"From the point of view of the clients, it looks very difficult to reeducate suppliers, doing magic with the forecast or reducing the lead times."

"Why do you say it is difficult for them to reduce the lead times?" Bill never runs out of questions.

"If they order more frequently, their administrative costs are much higher for all the people required to order many items to many suppliers in small quantities. Besides, these small quantities are usually smaller than the minimum quantities that we, the suppliers, will request." The devil is always in the details.

"Why do you request such minimums?"

"Bill, I know that we should be open to alternatives, but now you are ignoring the ABCs of manufacturing. Don't you know about the EOQ, economic order quantity? You need minimum batches to have economies of scale, right?"

"Richard, even if I agreed, you don't need to force all your clients with minimum quantities because you can get those quantities adding all the orders coming from several clients. This is not a good reason."

"But they still have the hassle of ordering too many items from too many suppliers."

"Fine, it looks hard and cumbersome. Much better if we can do it simply. But look at the consequences of reducing the order lead time to only one day."

"One day! I thought you were thinking of something reasonable!"

"Just imagine what would happen if your clients replenish every day only what was sold that day."

"Their inventories would be much less, I believe that the surplus wouldn't be a problem anymore, and besides the shortages would be solved much faster. It is very good, but the clients are the ones that decide what, when and how much they will buy. I don't see how I could convince them to change." This is one of those brilliant ideas that nobody can put in practice.

"Richard, all those are just obstacles! My claim is that if your company offers a service that ensures fewer inventories coupled with better availability, automatically you are in a blue ocean. Your clients will adore a service that increases their profitability so directly. What do you think?"

"I think that this idea is not new at all, but many companies tried and failed."

"You mean like the ideas presented in the book about blue oceans?" Bill is staring at me significantly.

"Okay, but unless we can see clearly how to do this practically without risks, it is nothing but a pie in the sky."

"I agree. It's time for the beers. Do you want to examine this idea tomorrow in the morning? I can use the Saturday for you if you are willing to work on it."

"Fine, only in the morning because we already have organized a barbecue with the family. You are invited if you want."

"Thanks, I'd like to but I also have a plan with the family. Let's go now."

I try to digest all what we have done today. I changed my understanding of what a strategic plan is. If Bill is right and we can make this idea fly, then only one thing will guide our actions in the next months. And now I see how that long list of important things will be reduced *dramastically* (both drastically and dramatically). I can hardly wait for tomorrow.

XIII

I woke up this morning with a strange sense of clarity that I had forgotten. I know exactly what we need to do, however I don't have a clue of how to do it, but the fact that Bill looked so confident last night energizes me.

We already have our coffees and Bill starts the meeting without more preambles.

"Richard, it is essential that we don't lose focus. I want you to summarize all we did yesterday, please."

"Yesterday we concluded that all our current issues in all areas are connected to a root conflict. Basically, we are always struggling to protect our current operation with some short term action. We also try to plan for future growth, except often the actions for that contradict the first ones. I understood that as long as we don't eliminate the conflict, all our issues will continue to appear, no matter how hard we work on them. We solve some for a while just to provoke others to reappear." After the battle everything is all so clear, isn't it?

"That is an excellent summary of the problem, which is, by the way, the same for many other companies. And if I know you well, you are not just saying this to please me, right?" We both laugh. Bill knows me very well. I continue the summary.

"After realizing that the conflict was the mother of all problems, we tried to invalidate some of the assumptions in the cloud. And we had a brilliant idea of creating a situation where competition is irrelevant, what they called a blue ocean."

"By the tone of your voice I see that you think these brilliant ideas are not always possible, right?"

That is exactly what I was thinking. "It is just hard to believe that it is always possible to create these blue oceans."

"Why? I mean, do you believe that knowledge is infinite?" Bill started philosophical again, I better focus him.

"Yes, but I want to be practical."

"Well, based on the facts that knowledge is infinite and our knowledge is limited, I conclude that all the knowledge of all mankind together is nothing compared to what it is yet unknown. Disturbing thought?"

I never thought about this before. The conclusion is clear and I dare to add more. "The unbelievable would be then that it is not possible to create a blue ocean in some cases... okay, you won also this one." Bill is smiling but with a different expression that I will not try to decipher now.

"So Richard, how did we end the day yesterday?"

"Oh yes, the brilliant idea for my company was to imagine a service where our clients would increase their turns, with significantly fewer inventories and much better availability. If they sell more, we sell more. And of course, we'd increase our market share by offering such incredible service. But frankly, I don't see how to do it."

"Thanks, that was a perfect summary. First thing to realize is that your perception of difficulty on the verge of impossibility to build such service is exactly the component that makes it hard to imitate. In this case we are not creating a new market but new conditions in the current market that will create blue waters around you. Today we must look at what it is necessary to build in order to create this blue ocean for your company."

"Maybe we should start with a study of the actual inventories in our clients' locations." I want to make this grounded and connected to reality.

"Richard my friend, we already know that piece of information. We know it by logic, because of the symptoms that you observe every day." Bill has a point. All these studies would take time and money just to confirm what we already are reasonably sure of. I wait, quiet, restless.

"Knowing that we need to offer such service we need to think of all the obstacles that prevent us from offering it today. Can you think of some obstacles?"

"That's easy. We can't force them to accept our deliveries in the time and quantities that we want. And also I see very difficult to manage the production if we are changing the production plan with every single change in demand. And finally, we don't want to increase our freight costs too much."

Bill goes to the board, erases it and writes two bullet points: 'Building logistical capabilities' and 'Building commercial capabilities'.

"Basically we need to see the changes required in your operations, both logistical and commercial. I want to start with production and distribution, is it okay with you?"

"You are the boss." I feel comfortable now with the process and confident that we are progressing toward something very interesting.

"To start looking at what to change in production, I want to introduce the principles of flow, because any production is about flow of material through a process. Did you read the article that I sent you last night?"

"I'm sorry, I saw the mail but I was too tired to read anything last night." That was honest.

"You always can read it, don't worry. The article was *Standing on the Shoulders of Giants*[2], written by Dr. Goldratt. I want to summarize the concepts of that article and take it from there." I nod and Bill goes to the board and writes down 'Principles of Flow' underlined, and below he writes four bullet points. He reads the first one aloud.

"Improving flow is a primary objective of operations. Do you agree with this statement?"

"Of course I do." Who wouldn't, I thought.

"Before you rush to agree, consider that anything that contradicts that statement should be rejected. The question is

_____

[2] Standing on the Shoulders of Giants, E.M. Goldratt (2008), it can be found in internet, some sites:
http://www.goldrattschools.org/pdf/shoulders_of_giants-eli_goldratt.pdf,
http://www.youtube.com/watch?v=C3RPFUh3ePQ,
http://www.scielo.br/pdf/gp/v16n3/v16n3a02.pdf (Gest. Prod., São Carlos, v. 16, n. 3, p. 333-343, jul.-set. 2009),
http://business.management6.com/Standing-on-the-Shoulders-of-Giants-Production-concepts-versus-download-w3461.pdf,

whether, as obvious as it sounds, you want to adopt this principle to guide your operations."

I must think a little bit more then. I can't find the catch. It is obvious that the operations are there primarily to make materials flow through them.

"If you are insisting on this now, is it because other people would not agree with it?" I want to be sure that I'm not missing anything important.

"Oh, I don't know anyone that wouldn't. But at the next minute they can be taking actions to obstruct the flow of production." As my face shows confusion, Bill continues, "Of course, that wouldn't surprise you now that you understand at what extent good managers are used to live within a conflict."

"Okay, so this is just a warning."

"Yes and a way to focus the conversation on only one thing." I nod for him to continue.

"If improving flow is our objective, we must try to remove all the major obstacles to flow, starting with the biggest. Do you know what is it?"

I try something knowing that I will get answers sooner or later. "I guess the bottlenecks."

"Bottlenecks are resources that don't have enough capacity for the demand placed on them, but they are not obstacles. The best way to understand this concept is using a very familiar situation. Have you driven on a clogged street? How would you compare the flow there to when there are half as many cars?"

"I see, the street might have a bottleneck that wouldn't obstruct the flow. So the biggest obstacle to flow is the excess of cars, right?"

"More precisely, the biggest obstacle to flow in any situation is the excessive work in progress or WIP. So the second principle comes from this fact: This primary objective should be translated into a practical mechanism that guides the operation when not to produce (prevents overproduction). In other words, we need a mechanism to control WIP up to a certain level."

"It sounds logical." I don't see how we should change anything in production yet.

"Consider now a typical process, like the street or a manufacturing process. The bottleneck is usually not the first resource, right?"

"Knowing that a generic process can have many resources, I agree that it is very unlikely that the first resource is the bottleneck, at least it is not the generic case."

"Then, if we reduce the entrance of WIP per unit of time, it is very likely that many resources will receive so little material that they will run out and stop working!"

"Now I see where you are going. These resources will have either idle time or they will slow down to try to look busy." I have seen this phenomenon before and I attributed it to laziness. Now I am learning to understand that bad behavior is caused by a conflict.

"But Bill, as I have seen this before in our production, we may be doing some WIP control already."

"Tell me something, Richard, when you see someone idle, what is it your reaction or feeling?"

"I feel that we are wasting capacity and I tell our production manager that we need to improve our efficiencies."

"The third principle is local efficiencies must be abolished, precisely to avoid these actions that only put pressure to increase the WIP." Finally the point emerges. The profound change is to stop measuring productivities at each work center. It is daring.

"If we give up all those measurements, how are we going to incentivize our workers? How are we going to calculate our costs?" I try to understand whether this is not just a partial view that ignores very important aspects of managing a company.

"You don't need local incentives or any unit cost to run your company."

I think for a while and say. "You are saying that many courses at the university are completely wrong, do you realize of that?" I want to be sure that I understood what I understood.

"I do, so what?" Bill looks a little bit arrogant now. "Before you call me arrogant, I will remind you again the story about Mendel and the inheritance laws. Can you show me any mistakes in all the logical derivations so far?"

"Not really, but it's hard to believe that so many teachers and professionals are wrong and have been wrong for so long. And more so, remember that we continue to use this as the standard, this is what the convention in our industry is, hell, it is the convention almost everywhere."

"When I first read *The Goal* my first reaction was exactly this same one. But the logic was so clear, the whole book was so full of common sense that it took me one minute to accept that I had had many wrong assumptions at the base of my so-called operations knowledge. That was sixteen years ago and I haven't found any reason to regret my decision yet."

Bill continues, "Anyway, you probably have seen many theories coming from the Toyota Production System, like just in time, later called LEAN, with several derivations like Quick Response Manufacturing or POLKA."

"I've heard of Toyota and LEAN only."

"It doesn't matter; there are many manufacturing theories that preach the WIP control mechanism to improve flow. The problem is that none of them emphasizes on the consequences of the actions taken to reduce the unit cost, for example."

"I've heard of failures implementing LEAN, is that the reason?" I'm interested because last year a consultant almost convinced me to implement it here.

"Not quite. Read the article and you will see there the reasons why LEAN doesn't work in the majority of production environments, and all of them stem from the variability in three aspects: demand, load and processes."

"Okay, so local efficiencies are not important. I want to know what to measure instead."

"We will look at your specific case in a minute. The last principle is a focusing process to balance flow must be in place. In other words, a mechanism to continuously improve flow is required."

"We are back to the conventional, everyone is preaching continuous improvement."

"Richard, you must understand that all those managers and teachers that you mentioned are very intelligent people. All their objectives are also mine. I don't agree with their tactics because of the wrong assumptions. That's all."

It was only forty five minutes ago that I thought different about production. I'm tired already. "Bill, come, I think we need cappuccinos before we continue."

XIV

Bill starts. "The principles of flow are generic and universal. We must now review the application of these principles that better suit your specific situation."

As I look confused, Bill says, "Do you know what the principles of driving are?"

"Well, moving the wheel, pushing the gas..."

"That's driving a car, right? But the principles are generic. I will give you what I think and you tell me whether you agree or not. To drive a vehicle you need only two principles; controlling direction and controlling speed."

"Correct. The application is the actual procedure depending on the vehicle. It is different for a car or for a submarine, right?"

Bill nods, "Fine, knowing that, we need the procedures to manage the flow in at least two operations in your company, production and distribution. I want to start with distribution first."

"I don't follow. Today we ship whatever the clients buy. What else do we need?"

"Yesterday we concluded that by replenishing only the consumption more frequently we would reduce inventory and we would improve availability. Do you have any regional warehouses?"

"We have two, at locations far from here."

"If you hold inventories at your plant warehouse, what is the transport time to those?"

"Three days by truck."

"Do you know how much stock do you hold today at those locations?"

"Yes, I do. It is a policy that we started last year to reduce our inventories. We aim to hold one month at each warehouse."

"Since the transport lead time is the only component of the supply lead time, you probably hold one month, because each item is replenished according to a MIN/MAX procedure, to ensure the economic batches, etc."

"Yes, we have set the maximum to replenish up to a month worth of sales and we only trigger a replenishment order when the stock goes below the minimum.

"How frequently do you send trucks there?"

"We send trucks almost every day."

"Knowing only that, I can tell you that you both have too much of most items and frequent shortages of some items at the regional warehouses. Right?" I'm almost taking an exam here, but all this is interesting for me, especially for the prospect of reducing my inventories without compromising on sales and, as I nod, I'm sure my face shows my frustration. Bill continues, "Furthermore, the MIN/MAX triggers a new order based on the physical level. But the consumption is variable; therefore the order lead time is also variable. Now you have a situation where the MAX is always wrong because it depends on a variable replenishment time."

I can understand and complete this reasoning. "Yesterday we saw that the inventory level should be the maximum forecasted consumption within the replenishment lead time. If this is variable, whatever level that we choose is wrong!" It is so logical, how come everybody keeps using that flawed procedure? "Let me see if I understand well. You propose to replenish daily only what was consumed from each warehouse every day. Is that correct?"

"Yes."

"But there are items that are sold in very small quantities, do you still think is economically viable to send them every day?" I don't want to overlook important aspects like freight costs. Maybe Bill doesn't care but I do!

"You said that you send trucks almost every day to each regional warehouse. I'm sure that you don't send them empty, and I also know that there is no infinite accumulation of stock at the warehouse. Then, my conclusion is that you are selling every day almost a full truck. Do you have any policy that forbids mixing much more variety in the same truck?"

Bill wins again. "We don't, and now I see your point. Actually doing this we would be sending to our regional warehouses only the items as they are pulled by the market."

"Very well put, it is a switch from push to pull. But you need to recalculate those maximum levels according to the new replenishment time of three days. In TOC, we call them buffers."

"Buffers? Like the car shock-buffers?" Nice jargon.

"They work exactly as car shock-buffers, absorbing the variability of the road to protect the car and to make your trip more comfortable."

"So these buffers are the quantities that we hold at the regional warehouse to serve a demand with fluctuations, right? It is the whole inventory including the safety stock."

"I couldn't say it better. Now you can see that the concept of buffer is the safety to be prepared for the unexpected."

"I don't follow." Bill is losing me here.

"The uncertainty of consumption means that from time to time the demand is much higher than expected and you are short of the item at the regional warehouse. What happens then?"

"Many times we order an urgent shipment from our plant warehouse… The buffer protects the system from these urgencies!"

"I would say mission accomplished. We finally saw how TOC, with simple tools, can eliminate the causes for the urgent."

"Don't you dare to stop here!", I laugh while I realize that he is absolutely right. With that cloud to solve the misalignments between authority and responsibility we solve the poor empowerment; with the cause and effect analysis and finding the root cause, we solve the long list of important issues; and the buffer concept solves being unprepared for the unexpected. This should be taught to all MBAs!

"Don't worry, unless you stop, I am willing to finish what we started." I didn't need the reassurance.

"Now that you need fewer inventories at both regional warehouses, you may want to take back a good deal of inventories to the plant warehouse. And you also need to recalculate the buffers at the plant warehouse. If you didn't have one, you need to get one, either renting or building." Bill waits for me to assimilate.

"Hey Bill, if I take back all that excess of inventory, my plant warehouse will be packed!" This is one of my current problems and I don't want to worsen it.

"It is possible, but it is necessary. However, consider that consumption from the plant warehouse will aggregate all the sales of the company," Bill says and goes to the board. He draws four boxes with a graph showing a highly fluctuating pattern, and a bigger box in the middle.

"Look, consider that these four boxes are points that you serve with your plant warehouse, this bigger box here," he then shows the graphs, "You see, these fluctuations force high buffer levels to ensure availability in each point. But take two and you see that fluctuations average out; the more points that you aggregate, the smaller the fluctuation."

"I already had reached this conclusion. So my plant warehouse should need much lower buffers compared to the current situation. But I still have problems of shortages at my plant warehouse. Why?" I knew this long ago and I couldn't understand it.

"The fact that you have a plant warehouse is not sufficient to aggregate the sales. As long as your clients continue buying based on their forecasts, you will only receive erroneous information to plan replenishment. Now you have the opportunity to test this new concept with two warehouses that you control." Bill waits for me while I think, it is not that easy.

"Fine, but the surplus inventories at the regional warehouses today are more than our current capacity in the plant warehouse." I need to be careful with these decisions.

"Richard, it doesn't make sense to take back all the excess just to replenish some of it the next day. The usual decision in these cases is to take back all the items that exceed more than double of the calculated buffers at the regional warehouses. Even in this case, you may need extra capacity for a while at the plant warehouse."

"That could work," I say more hopeful than convinced.

"And the buffers at the plant warehouse would be lower as well," says Bill.

I try to connect the dots. "Now, replenishment time is just production time, correct?"

"Correct, and you need to trigger frequent production orders. For example, weekly orders, corrected by technical batches."

"What does it mean?"

"It means that your plant warehouse replenishes your regional warehouses every day and registers each shipment as consumption in the plant warehouse. Once a week, all the weekly consumptions for an item add together, issuing a production order for the item to replenish the plant warehouse. If the quantity of the order is less than the minimum technical batch, you must correct the order to this quantity. Minimum technical batch means that a lesser quantity would do harm to a machine or a specific process couldn't be performed."

"On average, the inventory actually using space of the plant warehouse will be between one and two weeks; the rest will be WIP in production. So it is possible that we start packed, but that will be temporary. Besides, our plant will be able to catch up very fast with all the shortages in this period due to the lack of orders for the items already over buffer." Bill nods and stays quiet. I appreciate that he allows me to think and recap.

"So summarizing, the first step is to replenish actual consumption in the regional warehouses and the plant warehouse. With that we are controlling WIP and improving flow." Bill nods to everything. "Is that all?"

"That is the mechanism to move the goods, but you still need a mechanism to balance the flow when demand fluctuates. You need to adjust the buffers according to the trends."

"Finally! We can use our forecasting software for that!"

"You could, but I have a simpler suggestion." Bill goes to the board and erases it. He draws a vertical rectangle and writes the word 'buffer target' close to the upper left corner. "For each item at each location we will have a buffer target. The quantities on hand at the location plus the quantities on transit plus the consumption since last order should be equal to this target."

"Let me see if I understood. Just after an order, the quantities on hand plus all the ordered quantities are equal to the buffer. In other words, the replenishment order should complete only the buffer, correct?" I know that this is exactly what we already said, replenishing only the consumption, but now we are relating it to the buffer.

"Exactly. The consumption fluctuates, but if the average over time is the same, this method will ensure stability on the system. But the question is what happens when demand increases or decreases." Bill waits for me to answer.

"When demand increases, the stock on hand is less and less. And when demand decreases, the stock on hand remains close to the top of that rectangle." I like simple explanations, without complicated formulas.

"TOC proposes a very simple method to adjust the buffer target when demand shows a growing trend or the opposite. As you said, a growing demand will be manifested in low levels on hand. If we assign the color red to the first third of the buffer, when the buffer is red for too long we can understand that the buffer should be bigger, it is a signal that we are at risk of having a shortage. The method advises to increase the buffer equivalent to one third of the current buffer quantity." As he explains, he draws two lines dividing the rectangle in three equal zones and he writes 'red' in the lowest.

"Very clever, instead of keeping records of the danger zone for each item with numbers we just paint the first third with red, whatever the buffer is."

"When demand decreases, the on hand will be too much to protect availability. The upper third is assigned with the color green, when the on hand is always green during one replenishment time, the method is to reduce the buffer by one third. Of course, the on hand will be over the new green for a while. No replenishment order should be issued while the on hand is over the green. This is the way to reduce inventory when demand decreases." And he writes 'green' in the upper box.

"I guess that the middle third means stability. Is it yellow?"

"Yes, following a non written rule of using green, yellow and red. When the on hand is zero, the item is stock out, and then the color is black." He completes 'yellow' in the middle box.

I think for a moment and speculate an explanation. "This method is just like the simplest forecast formula, the moving average, isn't it?"

"That is correct. When we replenish only the consumption we are assuming that the immediate past will repeat in the immediate future. With buffer adjustments we just follow the trend as in the moving average."

"This is amazingly simple. Does it always work? I mean, there are no more surpluses or shortages?" I suspect that the method needs more details, but I like the simplicity.

"Of course it won't work in abnormal situations, where the demand fluctuates in huge intervals. There are also other considerations when the buffer target is much smaller than one unit. And of course all the known information should be an input to the system, like for example in Christmas season. But yes, it worked beautifully in all the places that we've done it."

"What else should I know about distribution?" I don't want to miss anything.

"We already discussed the replenishment mechanism, the dynamic buffer management, and why costs are not growing. The only question now is how to manage production, right?"

"If we do this, what do you think we can do with our new forecasting software?"

"I don't think you want to hear the answer." Bill laughs, and adds, "Don't do anything. You always can use it. There are some rare occasions where I would use good software to produce forecasts, but I don't want to deviate now to exceptions."

"Okay, another cappuccino and we can finish on time for the family lunch.

XV

We still have an hour and I already feel that we've gone very fast. Distribution was embarrassingly simple, but production is another story, with all the complexity of the machines. I don't think we can make it today. We are back and ready to continue.

"Now we need to know what to do with production. Again, the only thing that we need is to plan what to do and control the execution." Bill looks as if he is waiting for something. "Well?", he says.

"What, is that all?" I don't understand what he wants.

"I think that you can tell exactly what the plan is, how to execute it and how to control it."

"I can tell you what we do now. We have schedules for the machines to optimize the utilization of our capacity and we control that through daily production reports."

Bill is not impressed. "Tell me if I'm wrong, but I'd say that your daily reports show frequent deviations from the plan, to the extent that you must change the plan even daily."

"Of course we do that. This is the real world, where you must adapt to reality."

"And I also guess that you have some emergencies that change the plan from time to time." Now I'm not impressed. This is the very well known world of manufacturing, where uncertainty makes it very difficult to manage, and everyone knows it, including Bill.

"If we go now to the floor, how many machines are standing idle?"

"Hopefully none! But you know how it is. Anyway, our productivity is relatively high and we have worked on improving it with some success."

"Thank you for your patience. You know why I ask all the questions. I need to validate some facts before I can tell you whether you need changes or not. You definitely need some, but don't worry, it is also simple as in distribution."

"I thought you would need to know how the process was." I don't want that Bill will draw erroneous conclusions.

"Look, in production you have two different set of procedures; the procedures to actually do the transformation of material and the procedures to manage the resources. I can help you with the second set and for that I don't need any details of the first set now."

I'm not convinced yet, "What if we need minimum batches?", I ask recalling what we already discussed.

"I'm sure that you will raise it when appropriate and besides, we already said that you must adjust the production order size to minimum technical batches. To manage the resources you need an application derived from the four principles of flow. Afterwards we can discuss the details in your specific case." I nod to let Bill move on.

"I will remind you of the four principles of flow: improving flow is the primary objective of operations; there must be a mechanism to control work in progress or WIP; local efficiencies must be abolished; and a focusing mechanism must be in place."

"We used them in distribution. Is it the same in production?"

"Almost, there are slight differences. In distribution we control WIP setting a buffer and just replenishing what is consumed," Bill says.

"But we already said that production orders will be triggered only to keep the buffers full at the plant warehouse."

"Correct. Now I want you to consider that production lead time depends on the flow. We can safely guess that flow will increase when you control WIP, then the buffer levels for the items should be calculated with a shorter production lead time. Half of the current should be safe." Bill goes slowly and I thank him for it.

"So buffers at plant warehouse should be calculated as if replenishment time is already half of the current, is that right?"

Bill nods and says, "Production is the supplier for the plant warehouse, where we have our first buffers for the finished goods. In your case, where you produce to provide availability of the goods, the WIP control mechanism is exactly this, reducing the original targets. Then, production orders are only issued when there is consumption in the plant warehouse. And of course, these orders are corrected by the technical batch size and also by the adjustments decided by the dynamic buffer management mechanism that we already discussed before."

"That's it?" I know Bill, he started with the essence but there is more.

"You are right, triggering production orders just to replenish consumption in the plant warehouse is the planning mechanism. To control the right sequence we provide only one instruction to everyone on the floor. Follow the color code system; red is the highest priority, then yellow and green is the lowest."

"How do we know what orders are red or yellow or green?"

"We set it according to the color of the buffer in the warehouse. When there is more than one order for the same item in production, the first order takes the current color of the buffer, the second takes the color of the buffer as if the first was already delivered, and so on."

It makes perfect sense. We wouldn't release more material than the required to replenish the buffers in the warehouse. I complete my thought aloud, "And we are not using our capacity for things that we don't need."

"Exactly. Can you see all the ramifications of such decision?" Bill is expectant.

"I see positive effects in terms of correcting the inventory. What do you mean? Are there more?" I'm happy with this one. I wonder what I'm missing.

"Think of the consequences for the first resource and many others in your plant. What is the common practice today?"

"You mean they will be idle, don't you? I noticed that but frankly my dear, I don't give a damn." Bill laughs in relief and says, "I hope nobody will be gone with the wind of change though."

"It is clear that for me now that using our capacity to produce what we don't need is a real waste. I can change all our productivity measurements right away and I can adapt to abolishing local efficiencies understanding that we want to protect the global efficiency."

"Fine, you can do that, but I advise you to involve your operations manager in that decision." Bill is right, I better delegate these changes to the head of operations. "And the sequence will follow the real need of the items in the warehouse."

"Right, I like it because all the operators and supervisors will know exactly what to do without asking anyone else." It is so simple!

"Okay, we can leave now for our respective family reunions." Bill is already at the door and I am putting all my notes in a drawer. I need more time to review them before approaching other managers but I feel that finally we can do something that makes sense.

XVI

It took a week of meetings and some Skype calls with Bill, who was out of the country, but finally all the involved are executing the actions in production and in the regional warehouses. 'All the actions' is a mouthful because actually we just started two actions and stopped several. All of us have more free time now.

In the last two weeks, since we sent back to the plant from our regional warehouses everything that exceeded twice the buffers, our plant warehouse and regional warehouses had almost all the buffers full, with much less inventory in the regional warehouses. We cancelled all the production orders that were not needed and we could stop without any waste, and as we are just replenishing consumption for the few items below green, all the shortages were solved very fast. And besides, the inventory in the plant warehouse is also decreasing. Our CFO told me yesterday that we recovered a lot of cash and we could repay the line of credit extended by the bank recently. This was unexpected for me, but it's just great news.

For the first time in years, we are serving all the orders from clients in full. There are no more urgencies coming from clients because of our low fill rate.

Now we are dealing with extra orders from clients to cover their shortages. As a result, sales are also growing. Last week was 10% up. My guess is that solving the 5% of shortages at the plant warehouse, sales should grow about 5% as well, and the 10% was only a refill of the pipeline, but it won't last for long. We'll see.

I am thinking on what we discussed with Bill regarding that blue ocean thing. We are much better off now, and our clients are receiving an extremely good service. How can we possibly significantly improve this situation?

As Bill arrived last Saturday and staying for a week, I asked him to come tomorrow to discuss this with me. I really need to understand well what is going on and where his confidence does come from. My hope is that he will have a good surprise for me.

***

Bill is always on time, sharp. As he comes to my office I already asked for coffee.

"Hola amigo, how are you? I like coming over for these cappuccinos", I'm glad he is in a good mood because I plan to abuse his expertise this morning.

"How was the trip?", I ask politely as we sit.

"Never better, we discovered new things regarding the commercial process in one of our implementations. I believe that we should expect a rapidly growing flow of sales coming in because of the changes that we introduced there."

"What do you mean? You discovered that some things were not being properly implemented?" I learned to clarify my understanding before drawing conclusions.

"Not quite. We discovered, or at least we think we did, why sales were moving so slowly. There were issues both in the commercial process and in the way they presented the offers."

"Bill, I thought that after all these years those things would have been solved. Sales weren't growing before?" I'm worried if all these new actions are not effective enough yet, as I painfully worry about our own situation... I hope it's just me being too paranoid.

"Oh, that; don't misunderstand me. Our client was doing better than before, with a 20% to 30% hit rate compared to the less than 10% with which we started. But I wasn't comfortable with such low figures. After all, do we really believe that these blue ocean offers create such huge value? Do we?" Bill sips his coffee and adds, "If we really do, then we should expect a much better performance. And we should focus only on the anticipated value that we claim to create in the interaction with clients, otherwise the impression is that the offer only improves the service but they still bargain for prices and other conditions."

"That sounds pretty obvious to me, focusing on the value." Bill interrupts me.

"Yes, it is obvious! But salesmen are not used to blue ocean offers so they try to please the prospects in all the other aspects as well, to reinforce the message, it is what they are used to do. However, every time that they speak about other aspects, the message is diluted as if whatever thing different from the main concept on which the offer is based, is added on, it becomes a thinner, like watering the soup."

"Bill, I don't want to be rude, but that sounds pretty obvious to me."

Rather than taking offense, Bill smiles at me and says, "Thank you, my friend. 'Obvious' is the best praise for good logical thinking. I learned this from Eli himself."

"Okay, but still, that should have been pinpointed before, don't you think?" I want to understand whether this is laziness or something else.

"Richard, I will not try to explain things. I just want you to realize that this case is one where you see how our knowledge is nothing compared with what we still don't know. I'm surprised when I don't learn or discover something new monthly."

Fascinating, always open to new things, and at the same time, all the old knowledge is a solid base to build stable processes.

"Congratulations then!", I say while I raise my coffee.

"Thanks, what did you want to discuss today?" Bill is all business now.

"It's funny that you had this revelation last week. I want to discuss with you some doubts that I have regarding the blue ocean offer that you suggested some weeks ago, remember it?"

"Of course I do. The whole idea was to offer your clients a service that would increase their inventory turns to unbelievable levels. By the way, you haven't told me what happened here, in your warehouses."

"You surely remember our last conversation on Skype, how I had some troubles helping the operations manager to convince the warehouse managers and production manager to accept the new actions. That game that you taught me, with dice and chips, did all the magic. Finally, we took three trucks back from the regional warehouses, at no extra cost because after their deliveries they would have returned empty anyway. Now both regional warehouses and plant warehouse have availability of all our items. Inventory at regional warehouses is less than half while at the plant warehouse it increased for a while. We had to rent a container for a week. But as we didn't issue more production orders for the items over the green level, last Monday we returned the container and the warehouse is back to normal. Actually, I see that we gain room day by day, as the surpluses are consumed."

"So you could release cash in the last two weeks, couldn't you?" I like Bill's approach; 'show me the money'.

"You bet! And we are now cleaning up many areas of the shop floor. People gained time to think of better ways for many things like setups or methods. It was a good experience for everybody."

"Good stuff. I would expect that soon you will receive some negative ramifications from the success. Haven't you reduced the overtime yet?"

"Of course we did, from day one. Some workers were not especially happy about that because they relied on the extra money. We studied the situation with the operations manager and we saw that we could afford to increase salaries now due to the better productivity in the plant and besides we designed a general bonus for everybody just based on throughput increase. We think that we surpassed all their expectations and I see happier faces as I walk the plant now."

"You already increased the salaries and promised the bonus?" Bill looks surprised.

"Not exactly. We communicated to everyone that we would do this starting next month if we kept inventories at least at the current level with no shortages. But people could figure out by themselves that things are better with less effort, and I'm sure that they do their research on the sales, so..."

"What happened to sales?"

"Well, sales grew 10% in the last two weeks. I believe it is due to fulfilling some back orders and some emergencies from clients. But as our shortages were 5%, I expect that on average sales will increase 5%."

"Richard, do you remember Pareto principle in statistics?" I wondered when Bill would raise some academic thing, but now I learned how practical he is, I want to see where he is going.

"Yes, 80% of the result is caused by 20% of the factors."

"Yes. It applies when resources or factors are independent. In your production and logistical processes, where resources are dependent, the flow is dictated by the constraint and other principles apply. I wanted to clarify that, but all your items in the warehouse are mostly independent one from each other."

I get it, "If that is true, it follows that 20% of the items produce 80% of the sales. We know that and that's why we try to always have full availability of the high runners, the most important 20%." I know that look, Bill is not impressed again.

"You are suggesting that your 5% of shortages were on items that are slow runners, belonging to the worse 80%, producing in total 20% of the sales. If that were the case, recovering that 5%, should have generated less that 2% of lost sales. How do you explain the other 8%? Especially when you told me about the surplus that your company pushed recently onto the clients with that promotion?"

Logic is logic, how can I fight it! But if he is right, this is good news.

"Okay, what do you think it happened then?"

"I don't know what the composition of your shortages was, but I know some things. You run out of an item only when you forecasted lower sales, so it is very likely that several of the sold out items were fast runners. I also know that 20/80 is just a name; Pareto himself explained that the proportion could vary from one situation to the other." Bill waits, I already have some ideas and I want to speak my mind.

"According to that, eliminating some shortages of fast runners' shortages would mean more that 30% increase. But as you pointed out, clients are still clogged with inventories of slow runners, so 10% was only a start of a trend."

"Very good cause and effect thinking", Bill teases me, "You will soon be able to think all by yourself," he says smiling and I don't take offense. On the contrary, he is right. I could have drawn these conclusions alone. I had all the data and the knowledge required to build this new knowledge on my own.

"Would you say that your clients are still suffering from shortages?" Bill asks, following the same line of thought.

"I don't need to guess, it is obvious from the emergency orders that they place between the regular ones."

"You can imagine that the same will happen to them when they solve their shortages, they will increase their sales." Bill is right, only that the increase would be different.

"Considering that my warehouses aggregate so much demand, my mistakes are smaller than the ones that our clients are making in their forecasts. And, all the increases in their sales will be in addition to the increase in mine!" Now I'm starting to see what means to suffer the negative effects from success. It is like the Chinese saying, 'beware of what you wish for; you might get it'.

"Five years ago I had a case of a company that solved shortages of 5% and their sales shot up by 40%!" Bill has extensive experience and what I thought it was an exception is the norm.

"Was it one of your clients?"

"It was a prospect. I went to an evaluation meeting to see whether we had something to offer them." Bill looks like he said too much already. But I'm curious and I stare at him, waiting for more details.

"Okay, this is the story. They did something incredibly daring, against all common practices, which I really admired at the time. They increased the inventories to the extent that all shortages were solved."

"For how long did they keep this policy? Are they bankrupt now?" I know the risk of tying up too much cash in inventories.

"Fortunately they stopped that policy after a year or so. But you are right, they had to write off a very big portion of their inventories two years later, taking a bit hit in profit."

"It sounds like a mistake, doesn't it?"

"It is a story about people incredibly courageous that proved two things. Solving shortages of 5% increased sales by 40%, against the common wisdom, like you told me before, all that mumbo jumbo about never letting fast runners run out."

"Now I understand and I hope you are right. The logic is sound. And what is the second thing?"

"That inventories are a liability, more than even you think. I bet that you believe that high inventories are a cash drain."

"Of course they are. Do you disagree?" What surprise does he have up his sleeve now?

"They are, and when the company runs out of cash, that's it. But before that, high inventories are operationally an obstacle to flow, remember?"

I think of the actions that we take to get rid of the surplus like promotions and the regular discounts and I do realize how our clients suffer from the same things.

"High inventories are obstacles for sales because the promotions to get rid of the surplus cannibalize the sales of the good items, correct?" Now I see another huge damage.

"Yes, that is one thing. Besides that, surplus ties up cash that prevents replenishing fast runners. The same happens with the space, haven't you had the situation of the warehouse packed and you had to stop production?"

"Yes, that too." It was much worse than I thought. "And to push surpluses out requires much better display, hurting even further the sales of other products."

"You probably introduce new products from time to time, to refresh the portfolio, don't you?" Bill has no mercy.

"Yes, I do. And, now that you mention it, clients are always trying to return obsolete items that should be replaced by the new ones, but I don't accept that, which makes them like us less. High inventories are devastating!" I must admit that it is much worse that I could have imagined.

"The story of that company is that they returned to the usual shortages and now they know what means to eliminate them. But their action led to worse results. I hope they will be open to discuss some alternatives with us, like the ones that you have been implementing. Fine. You were saying something about doubts regarding the blue ocean offer?"

Bill has this ability to touch the wound and it hurts but at the same time I'm glad to understand much better the power of this particular offer.

"That was one hour ago. I understand now that our clients cannot reduce both shortages and inventories at the same time without our help. And knowing the incredible effect on sales that both things would have, I really understand now how offering this service will solve our core conflict. I am starting to worry about capacity. But now my question is: what is the next step." Bill is smiling again.

"Well, regarding capacity, we must talk later. It is easy; the only thing that you need now is to convince your clients of accepting a collaboration deal where they give you their daily sales and you replenish them frequently, while you also adjust their buffers." Bill says this without a pause.

"Can you repeat the last part?"

"Which one?"

"From 'it is easy'", we both laugh. He is right again, by doing that, sales will be boosted and inventories will remain low. It would be a real beauty of a supply chain.

"Seriously, after our last promotion and the history of pushing inventories, I don't think they would accept such a deal so easily. I believe that it will take a long time. And by the time I convince them, a competitor could capitalize on the same idea. Bye, bye to our competitive edge."

"That is why you need to carefully plan four things: how to get appropriate prospects for this offer; designing a good offer; designing a good persuasion process; and applying the principles of flow to the sales process."

"Have you done this before?" I don't want to be a guinea pig.

"Before answering, have I asked you to trust me so far? I think that you trusted your intuition and your logic in all that you have done." That is correct; I'm still coming back to the old habits of judging an action by the acceptance of a group. As I nod, Bill continues.

"Yes, we have done it, successfully. And we learned valuable insights on the way." This is a reassurance that I appreciate.

"Look Richard, I need to go somewhere nearby for half an hour. You can clean your desk in the meantime. What do you think?"

"Perfect, we will still have two hours before lunch."

XVII

"Before we move to the commercial process, I want to ask you about capacity." I don't want this subject to be forgotten.

"Richard, today your throughput is determined by your ability to sell more, but the time will come when you don't have enough capacity for the new level of sales and you will need to expand it, and then the market will again be the bottleneck. It is a controlled oscillation. The ultimate constraint is always management attention, so now let us focus on the commercial part and later we will discuss the mechanism to prudently expand capacity, okay?"

I knew it, but at least now I have my answer. I nod and Bill takes a while, he is thinking.

"In operations you changed the way resources are managed, but there were no changes in the way they do the transformation or moving the goods. In sales we need both types of changes: managing resources and how to process the opportunities."

"I see, workers on the floor only see that we now release less WIP but we didn't tell them to change what to do with it. Changing habits is way more difficult, isn't it?"

"It is, and that's why the changes in the commercial process are harder to be fully adopted. On the bright side, though, it is the difficulty to imitate such changes that solidifies your edge for a longer period of time."

"That's good provided that we can do it in the first place," I say stating the obvious.

"It is not that hard if you focus your attention on the logic behind the communication. The same logical persuasion process that we need to teach the salesmen to do, you must use on them first. And we also need to apply the principles of flow to the 'pipeline management', like in a pipeline, opportunities flow through it, ending either in a sale or a failure."

"What do we do first?"

"I propose a general overview of the whole process and how to apply the principles of flow to it."

"Fine with me; besides, after applying them twice I'm feeling more comfortable with all this simplicity."

"Can you describe how it works today, from marketing to sales?"

"Today marketing is the area of the company that produces merchandising, manages the advertizing budget, and prepares promotions. They also go to the points of sale and see that our products are properly displayed."

Bill is listening and nodding. "Sales department has the task of looking for more opportunities, calling the current clients that are behind their average purchases, and processing all the purchase orders. On top of that, sales department produces and adjusts the forecast before passing it on to production. Of course, this is not true anymore for the last two weeks."

Bill is thinking and I add, "Of course this is just in a nutshell. There are much more details."

"Richard, could you tell me what are the objective of marketing and the objective of sales?"

When Bill starts with fundamental questions, I know that a paradigm shift is coming. I will try to guess the 'right' answer and hope to get the TOC answer sooner rather than later.

"Marketing is responsible for creating awareness, increasing the perception of value and managing all the communications with the market, especially advertising." Now I wait for Bill.

"In TOC we define things before we use them because the best way to confuse somebody is giving the same name to two different things. Marketing for TOC is a function that has one objective: generating demand. In other words, it answers two questions; what to offer and to whom."

"Isn't that what I said?" I want to understand the difference.

"Maybe, but we will use this definition which encompasses activities which are many times quite different from the common practice. Of course, we are not changing fundamental things here, only the way they are done. And what is the objective of sales?"

"Negotiating with clients the best deals possible and trying to get more clients."

"Very close to my definition, but again I will use a simple one: to convert the generated demand into money."

I think for a while and I realize how simple it is. I knew it all the time but sometimes confusion comes from that fog of complexity spread by well-intended people trying to control it all.

"I like them. We first generate demand and then we turn it into money. It couldn't be simpler. What now?"

"Now, knowing the idea that will create the blue ocean, we can do four things: prospecting, building the offer, designing a persuasion process and instituting a pipeline management procedure." Bill writes down these four elements on the board.

"So you are saying that we need a blue ocean idea before doing these things?"

"Richard, we need to focus everyone in the organization toward the same objective, otherwise the areas will behave as independent silos, seeking their local optima instead of one global optimum."

I think that I understand and say, "The idea for our blue ocean will guide all the activities in the company. Is that what you are saying?"

Bill nods and adds, "The whole company should strive to build, capitalize and sustain each of the competitive edges that you are pursuing. Today we are discussing the first one, offering better turn to clients."

My head is spinning, "According to this concept, we are now doing so many things that are not important at all, like, so many other companies that I know of... And now, I can see how simple is to manage the company without a long list of activities, we have simplified great many things, but is far from trivial."

"I don't mean to frighten you now but you will have to do a lot of work. However, there will be no more disconnected issues or activities. Everything is focused by the blue ocean idea.

On the other hand, you will probably free up a lot of time sooner than you think." Bill is back to the board and continues ignoring the expression on my face.

"Prospecting is mining information about the market guided only by the degree to which the need that you are satisfying is significant."

"Please, can you clarify this?"

"A blue ocean idea or a decisive competitive edge, as we call it in TOC, is gained when you can satisfy a significant need of enough clients at the extent that no other significant competitor can." Bill explains further without pause. "A significant need is not the most important one, it is something that today is not satisfied but when it is, the clients really appreciate the created value."

"In this case increasing turns could even be the most important need of my clients." I understand better and I want more clarity.

"It might be; the key is that the need is significant." I nod.

"Then, the whole idea is to provide a service that could increase turns beyond their imagination. Today your clients are struggling to increase their turns by even 20% and we are discussing how to at least double them."

"Definitely nobody would be able to offer such thing with the current mode of operation. I couldn't some weeks ago." This is powerful and now I get a glimpse of that simplicity that Bill has been talking about.

"Not only that. You know how to do it. You need two conditions; perfect availability at your warehouses and control over the inventories of your clients."

"My perfect availability wouldn't do much if they continue buying as they do today, correct?"

"That's right, so you need to convince them to report their daily sales and you replenish frequently, and besides you have to monitor and adjust their inventory levels with the dynamic buffer management system."

"Once we do this, what prevents our competitors from quickly imitating this service?" I can't believe that such a simple thing is not easy to imitate. Bill is smiling at me and after a while he speaks.

"You don't understand all the paradigm shifts that you've gone through, do you? And you already forgot that you needed several sessions with your production and distribution personnel to convince them of changing. And now you need to do the same with the entire commercial department."

"Okay, okay, understood. It is simple, but far from easy." I like it.

"The first thing to do is to decide how to look for prospects. What do you think we need?"

"Such an offer will be attractive to clients that buy inventory for resale."

"What are you going to do if someone wants a big order for some reason?" Bill is testing my understanding and I appreciate that he asked this question.

"We've had opportunities like that in the past, and we took them gladly. Now I think that we shouldn't because such big orders could deplete my warehouses of the products that I am supposed to replenish to consumption, jeopardizing the service on which we based our competitive advantage." Bill is staring at me.

"I couldn't have said it better," he says, "more precisely, if you allow your strategy to bend under any opportunity, you start zigzagging with the risk of turning sharply into a brick wall. You can read that in chapter five of 'Isn't it Obvious?', the last book written by Eli Goldratt." He looks at the board and says, "Excellent!, details can be decided by you and your team later on."

Then he goes to the board and points to the second bullet. "Designing a good offer is key, and here we need two elements: showing and enhancing the benefits for the client and your company; and setting terms and conditions that prevent possible setbacks for both, the client and your company."

I never liked tricks and say, "Of course, lots of fine print is out of the question, correct?"

"Correct, that could kill the most appealing offer. We need to show how this is a real win-win deal. And let me tell you what I understand by that. Win-win is only possible when there are two elements: mutual benefit and mutual commitment."

I like this approach. In the past, I thought big clients tried to abuse my company, under the name of win-win, asking for consignment, for example. Now I understand what I didn't like; no commitment from their side. "Good definition. I like it."

"Let us review the four elements, benefits and risks for both parties."

"Well, it is obvious the benefit for the clients; they will get more turns."

"True and that is the key element in the first presentation where we validate with the prospect the value of the new service. Now, don't forget your benefit, which is comprised by three elements; more volume, good prices and better cash flow."

I think for a moment. More volume is obvious; when clients sell more, we sell more. Regarding the prices, I'm sure clients will ask for discounts anyway. The interesting element that I didn't think of is the cash flow. "Do you think that we can reduce payment terms?"

"Why not? After all, your clients will be receiving much smaller quantities each time, obtaining their return much faster. I would say that nobody should have any problem with shorter terms to pay the smaller and more frequent invoices, using the additional cash they will generate."

"That would improve further our cash-to-cash cycle, beautiful. As for the prices, I'm sure clients will ask for discounts, don't you think?"

"Of course they will. They are conditioned to do it. But look how a big discount on price, let's say 10%, compares to doubling turns. Don't forget that your clients invest their money to get a profit, like an interest rate from an investment fund."

"That analogy is good. My brand is a fund and so are our competitors', if we can double the turns it is like halving the investment but still getting the same return. Now that I think in these terms, I see that we not only compete with other manufacturers doing similar products; we compete financially with all their vendors. The impact could be much higher, and we could –" Bill stops me for the first time in weeks. "I know that you are discovering more and more things. It is natural that you can build new things over a solid base, but today we should focus only on this."

I'm excited. The possibilities will be huge. But Bill is right, if I start considering more strategies, I will be back to bad multitasking.

"Agreed, the benefits are clear. What about the risks?"

"First, you should consider the risks for your clients, like being flooded by inventory. Don't forget that today your salesmen are still pushing it down the throats of clients."

"Okay, so we put ourselves in their shoes and think of all the possible risks for them and add elements to the offer that will trim them. What about ours, should we do the same?"

"You should think of all the risks for your company, like for example, the released cash and space not to be used on other goods. And then, when the prospects are excited, there is a meeting to discuss terms and conditions, where your people raise your company's concerns and let the clients speak. Most of the time clients come up with better solutions than you would have expected."

"Everything follows a logical process. I'm sure that we can decide the details of the offer with our commercial team." As I say this, Bill goes to the board and say, "Designing the sales process is one of the challenges in the whole plan. I would prefer to leave this for the last, so now we should discuss how to apply the principles of flow to the whole process."

"May I?" Now I have the confidence to try it.

"Please." Bill sits and I take the marker.

"The four principles were; flow is the number one consideration; we need to control WIP; local efficiencies must be abolished; and a focusing mechanism must be in place to balance flow. We already agreed on the first." I look for approval on Bill's face and as he nods I continue. "WIP in this case is the number of open opportunities that each sales person has. We could limit this number to an agreed limit, like fifteen. Only when one opportunity is won or lost, another is assigned to that person."

"Richard that is exactly what we have done in some implementations. People move the opportunities much faster because they don't have enough room for bad multitasking. The limit was ten in my experience, but it depends on the cycle time. Good, please go on."

"The third principle is to abolish local efficiencies." I try to understand where we have the local optima in sales. I'm thinking and Bill waits. As I seem to be confused, Bill asks a question, "Do you remember your productivity bonuses in production?"

"Those only lead to local optima! In sales we pay commissions per each sale! Bill, this is one of the most cherished compensation methods in any industry. Are you suggesting abolishing commissions?" Bill laughs and says, "Why not?"

Why not! This is too much. I study his face and he really means it.

"Richard, I will ask you some questions and from your answers you can draw the conclusions. First question: how will the salesmen collaborate to get a sale? Do you have any collaboration between them now?"

"You kidding? They pretend to be collaborating, but they compete with each other constantly. They even fight fiercely to get the accounts when a salesman leaves the company. We have a lot of problems reassigning accounts even when some of them are poorly served."

"Second question: which does a salesman prefer, a big account or a medium one?"

"Rhetorical questions? Of course the big one."

"So medium clients are poorly served as a consequence, right?"

"Maybe. So?"

"Do you like to depend on big clients for your business?"

"Okay, now I see. It is better to have many clients to avoid an imbalance in power, and becoming a victim of a giant."

"Now that you will tell each salesman, what to do, when and with whom, don't you see that the commission will put them in a permanent conflict of interest?"

"But they must obey, or else." I don't like smart cookies.

"Richard, salesmen are specialists in giving good explanations for everything. You trained them! With all the problems you've caused clients in the past, they know how to explain the unexplainable. You need their collaboration but not by forcing them, it will only bring more trouble and you risk increasing the disharmony in the group, not a recipe for success. We must do it differently."

Bill is staring at me. I'm thinking hard. This is a very deep change and I wonder how our people will take it.

"If we change their compensation scheme from base salary plus commissions to only a better salary, some of them will leave the company, the best ones, those that make the best commissions."

"What is the negative effect?" Bill is really irreverent, isn't he?

"Our sales will drop!"

"Why?"

"Because we would lose our best people who get the highest volumes!" As I say this, it hits me. We no longer will push volumes in single orders. "Wait, either they convert to the new game or they will be better off out of our company."

"Well put. You won't push anyone out, but you will neither beg anyone to stay. Never put your company in the situation of depending on a client, or a supplier, or an employee."

We've suffered in the past for ignoring such wise advice.

"I see why to abolish commissions and my understanding is just at the same level as my fear to do it."

"Of course you must plan this move very carefully. But let me tell you that our clients overestimated the negative effects, and the commercial teams embraced the changes gladly. Not only that, sales people are now part of the team and not a segregated tribe as before."

"And we could move them from one position to another if we required it. I like it."

"What about the fourth principle?" Bill reminds as I had forgotten everything with this injection of rebellion against the status quo.

"We need a mechanism to balance the flow, periodic meetings with each sales person to see what is going on with the open opportunities. I bet that these meetings would be much shorter and focused than the ones that we have today."

"That's true. It is also the experience of our clients. Now think of the actual procedures and what positions you need there."

"Let's see, we need someone prospecting, who will produce a list of prospects. And we need someone scheduling the time of salesmen, who will assign new opportunities from the list of prospects only when an opportunity is closed. We need people that can assist salesmen with paperwork and some technical visits, because we want them to use their time for nothing but nurturing opportunities, persuading prospects and bringing replenishment deals."

"I see that you read emails after all," Bill says. He included me in the internal report for the last week's visit. I might be interested. Of course now he caught me; that is how I could figure out myself the application from the principles of flow. Anyway, I think I did it pretty well just by heart.

"Fine, so you know what to do and we can discuss details when you and your team have decided them. Now it's late and we should have lunch. When can you continue with the persuasion process?"

"Accept my invitation to have lunch and we will work on it this afternoon."

"I thought you had things to do."

"I do, but this is the most important thing in my agenda now, to build and execute this plan as soon as possible. Would you stay?"

"I will, only because you asked so nicely."

XVIII

I order a couple of juices as a good companion for a light lunch, preventing "el burro" – (the donkey) this feeling of severely needing nap time once you have eaten well, without energy to think and just before needing to restart work. The body is busy dealing with the glucose and energy while the brain seems to be fully satisfied and in no hurry to engage in anything serious.

"Hey Bill, I'm curious, how come you or your company are not famous, or much better known by now?"

"What do you mean?" Bill asks casually, as if he really doesn't understand. I know he does. I stare at him for a moment and he speaks again with a voice and gestures that reveal that he understood.

"We are doing very well, there are thousands of companies in the world that are using TOC and we have dozens of good clients all over the world."

"Look, the kind of value that I am getting from you in such short time is way beyond anybody's expectation when talking to a consultant. Considering that in the afternoon we will discuss the persuasion process, I want to have your true hypothesis of why you don't have thousands of clients knocking on the door."

"Richard, deep change is a door locked from the inside. Nobody can force that lock, and the only thing we can do is call out from the outside, trying to be heard. Most people are so comfortable where they are that they don't think of moving to something else, even if you show them a potential treasure at the end of the rainbow. A pot of gold at the end of the rainbow is a fantasy for most of them."

"Very poetic, I'm impressed. But something like what we already did in less than a month is real and extremely valuable. My question is how come people don't see it?" This is a mystery, I don't buy the 'inside-locked' story.

"I use to think like that, my friend. Let me ask you a question: do you remember our first conversation some weeks ago?" I nod, knowing where this is going.

"If I remember correctly, you weren't particularly eager to analyze anything with TOC. And you've proved to be both open minded and as brilliant as always these last weeks. Why are you so surprised about TOC not being main stream yet?" I think for a while and before I can say another word, Bill continues.

"Do you remember what motivated you to accept my offer for the first session?"

"I was troubled, and I said that I didn't want to regret not trying everything at hand." It was not that I didn't know about Bill's claims of being able to do simple and powerful analyses before that.

"You see, what you felt was what we call the 'crocodile', a real threat that drives you to change. It is the negative of not changing."

"I guess there are negatives and positives of changing and not changing." Bill has this weird smile on his face again and waits.

"Everybody must have good reasons for not changing, their positives, like a warm blanket in their comfort zones."

"We call that the 'mermaid', a beautiful mermaid that you have now and don't want to give up." Bill says.

"Of course most of the people are trying to move on, to progress, and to improve somehow." I'm trying to understand these forces that make people move or stay.

"And as Eli said, every improvement is a change, but not every change is an improvement. That's why people study the pluses and minuses of changing or not. There must be a good enough reason to change, either running from the crocodile or, the least, trying to achieve a 'pot of gold'. The problem is that in any change there are risks, what we call the 'crutch'." Bill sips his juice as I digest what he is saying.

"I look back and I can see how content I was with our performance, and only when I perceived a real threat I was ready to try something new. Mmmmhh... now I understand what you are saying about business people. But academics should be different! They are supposed to search for the best methods, to develop better approaches to the problems we face and I'm sure this is not a secret for anyone, is it?" What am I missing?

"Richard, again you are ignoring a fundamental human behavior. Academia adopts new paradigms only after they are proven for many years and they are part of mainstream. They hate risks. Take for example the Gantt chart used for project management. Henry Gantt started using it for the first time around 1905. It was 1950 until a big project organization adopted it, and it was not popularized and taught in universities until the

70s. This is just another example in addition to the genetic laws and many others."

"But TOC surely is taught in many universities today, right?" I can't believe nobody is teaching it.

"It is taught in more than two hundred business schools that I know of, and most MBA programs give you The Goal as a mandatory reading, usually in operations. That doesn't mean at all that it is main stream. In all those schools you will find it taught alongside contradictory and even erroneous material, like cost accounting for decision making." I wonder if Bill says all this bitterly. If so, he doesn't show it.

"But all this doesn't explain why businessmen are not listening and adopting it much faster. Maybe you don't have good marketing?" Bill's face shows that I hit a sensitive spot.

"Well, that is my question too. For now, just saying that we can show a way to simplify management and that getting results beyond your imagination is possible with TOC has not brought a lot of clients. I personally think that the 'pot of gold' moves a few, but the real driver is the crocodile. But then, many times it is too late. We can successfully get through the message in long sessions, from one to four days."

"I guess that most managers don't have the time, do they?" Now I understand better.

"Good guessing." Bill says with the last drink of his espresso, "And we don't have many of those." I think for a while, he has been talking about Goldratt's books since we met.

"You know what?" I say hesitantly, "Maybe you and your colleagues should write books with your ample experiences. It is not only those seminal books written by the inventor; many other books would have wider effect. Don't you think?" I believe this is a brilliant idea, one I'm sure Bill will accept on the spot.

"I don't know. We already have Eli's books, besides there are many others that wrote TOC books. It is too much work, and I don't know whether I could significantly contribute more that others that are better than me. And I'm waiting for Goldratt's Wisdom, a book written by his son and his son in law as we speak." Oh my God!, the mermaid, the crutch, the absence of crocodile and pot of gold, all in one sentence. Now I understand.

"Bill, thanks for a good lesson on what resistance to change is", I grin at him. "Would you consider writing a book as a marketing tool?" I remembered that that door is opened from the inside.

"I will think about it, I promise. Shall we go?"

***

We asked for a couple of glasses of water while we sit. Bill seems to be putting order to his ideas and eventually he speaks.

"Persuasion is a combination of a logical analysis and an emotional presentation, leveraging on our interlocutor's intuition." He pauses and I just listen.

"We need to use a couple of logical tools to understand our prospect's environment better than he does, in order to prepare a good presentation. These tools are the four quadrants of a change and the layers of resistance."

"Are the quadrants the crocodile and mermaid thing?"

"Yes, exactly. We need to understand what the pot of gold and the crocodile are that would move someone. And besides we need to understand what the mermaid and crutches are that paralyze them. Okay, maybe 'paralyze' is an exaggeration, but you understand what I mean."

"So we build a matrix with the pluses and minuses of changing and not changing. I think I get it."

"Yes, do that, but from the perspective of your prospects."

It is simple, like the SWOT analysis, looking at strengths, weaknesses, opportunities and threats, but with other concepts in mind.

"You mentioned another tool, some layers."

"Yes, the layers of resistance are different obstacles to be overcome in the persuasion process. As always, this is just plain common sense." I know what that means; he will produce a rabbit from his hat, with a logical process that I didn't think of before.

"The primary layers in any change are three: what to change – the problem, what to change to – the solution, and how to cause the change – the actionable plan." I knew it was obvious. But I don't fool myself anymore with that word. Many times I have started with the solution or the plan, before defining clearly what the problem was.

"Each one of them has more layers. This is like an onion, you must peel off the layers one by one, and when you do, usually someone cries and there is a little stink." I laugh at the analogy. It is funny yet real as I consider it.

"The first three layers are: I don't have a problem; my problem is different; my problem is not under my control." Bill pauses for me to digest and I jump in.

"There is no point discussing a problem unless there is recognition of a problem in the first place. I think I got it."

"The second layers are: I have a different direction for a solution; the solution doesn't cover the whole problem; the solution could bring negative effects."

"What do you mean by direction?" Too much jargon can lose me.

"For example, you want to convince your clients to reduce shortages and one direction could be increasing inventories."

"That's crazy talk!"

"I know, but you see this is one direction. We know it is suicidal but it would increase sales for a while." Bill chooses good examples, looking at the extreme I understand better.

"The last layers are: there are obstacles to implement the solution; and disagreement with the details of implementation."

"Very clever, the discussion doesn't go further before the previous layer was not overcome."

"Well, that was the process before. However you will not be talking to robots. Human beings have emotions and they understand things very fast through intuition when you speak to them about a subject about which they have plenty of experience."

"How did it change then?" I was fascinated with the process and Bill tells me it is not good anymore. What's the deal?

"Don't misunderstand me. The whole work as before must be done. Salesmen must understand your clients' business better than they understand themselves, so the whole logical and detailed construction of the problem and the solution must be built."

"And what you say is that the presentation can be just a short one triggering the intuition of the people to recognize the problem and then welcome the solution, is that it?"

"It took me months to figure that out, my friend. That's exactly what I'm saying."

"Summarizing we could say that we need to train our sales people to understand exactly how low turns is a significant need of our clients. Then they need to learn how to show it with good enough images that will trigger frustration for the low turns. Then, we provide hope with our solution, and giving details that are feasible. Many prospects will be open to try it."

Bill is speechless. I thought that was not possible and I don't refrain from laughing, mainly because I can smell the sales rolling in.

I want more details. "When are you going to train my people?" I stare at him as he stands up and starts pacing my office.

"Look Richard, I really can't do that. I don't have the time, but it is much better if I teach you and you train your sales manager. Then accompany him to a couple of visits for him to experience firsthand the process. You must coach him closely until he is confident and becomes a champion of this new way. Only then he will lead the rest of the team, doing the same coaching each one at a time." As Bill speaks I can envision how we will develop our own internal capabilities. I like it much better.

"You convinced me," I smile at him. "Can we start the day after tomorrow? I really need to drain some more WIP from my list, which is getting shorter, but not gone yet. Thank you very much. Today it went beyond my expectations."

"My pleasure. I can't wait for your successes. And yes, the day after tomorrow is perfect, because I'm travelling again in four days time and I also need to fix some stuff before leaving."

XIX

It's been four months since my last training with Bill. Of course a biweekly Skype conversation was a key link in my education. Yes, I can call it an education in how to manage a company.

Inventories at our warehouses have never been lower, whilst the sales are growing like weeds. I am a little surprised with the speed at which clients are accepting our proposal. Of course, the bigger ones want a pilot and the cycle with them is slower. One of the biggest, representing fully 10% of our sales, insisted on bargaining our price, but as we had grown a good deal with many others, today they were only 3%. We stood firm on our price. Although I could tell they wanted the deal, they negotiated themselves into a corner. Seeing no way out without them losing face, we suggested that they try a competitor for a while to see if they can do everything we promised. Losing it was not a disaster. We have recovered most of the lost business already on more favorable terms. Besides, in three months we will present them our offer again and I bet they will accept it this time. It is good to feel free!

Our profit this quarter will end up being the best in our history. And best of all, our position is stronger than ever. In fact, we completely paid off our debt last month.

I don't have a list of pending issues anymore. I stopped receiving calls and complaints from my clients; this has been an important KPI for me to see the improvements. Harmony in the company has shown me that all these changes are congruent, they are the right things to do. From time to time I must take care of some problems that I will not delegate to anyone. But now I really have the time to think and plan the future.

Bill is arriving in town this afternoon and he accepted a dinner. I owe him so much, that's the least I can do.

***

"How was your flight?"

"It was the kind I like; uneventful." We sit and order some appetizers and drinks while we look at the menu to decide.

"What was it this time? Another workshop to market your services?" I ask half interested and half to start the conversation.

"This week I facilitated a process of two days and a half for a company that didn't have a clear blue ocean offer." Now I'm interested.

"What do you mean facilitated? You developed it, didn't you?"

"Oh, no! I just guided them through the process. You know, the UDEs from the market, the core cloud of their clients, the assumptions, and some exploration of ideas to invalidate any of the assumptions; the usual process."

"And what happened? Did you get anywhere?"

Bill hesitates a little bit and says, "At the beginning I had an idea in my mind and I was aware of the fact that I could be blocked by that. I tried to forget it and let the process flow with their input."

As the pause is longer than expected, I ask again, "Did you or did you not get a breakthrough idea?"

"We did! However, it was a weird experience." Bill is again hesitating, but this time I wait for him. Eventually he speaks again, "I am trying to understand whether we got to that simple, and now obvious, solution with the process or was it just the spark of someone's brilliance. I only remember that we had four ideas written on the board, showing how it would be beneficial for clients and what new capabilities were being considered. And discussing them, one said one thing, another said another thing, and suddenly, both the CEO of the company and I understood that we had arrived to the solution that we were looking for. By the way, the idea that I brought with me was not part of the solution."

"How did you know it was a good solution when you saw it?" I want to learn more about these thinking processes.

"I knew it because it evaporated the core cloud so simply and elegantly. However, I had to rewrite D and D' in a way that showed clearly how this idea eliminated the conflict."

"You mean it wasn't obvious from the original cloud? Did you manipulate the words?" I don't like tricks, I hope that we can have a strong process.

"I wouldn't say manipulated. In fact we used words that were more precise to express the same generic concept. That's why I'm wondering whether it was the process or we needed another process."

"For me it is clear that the solution came from the process. Come on! Two and a half days? That's incredible, man!" I'm not just cheering him up, I really believe that it is a very short time.

"I guess," Bill is somehow discontent.

"Do you really have to guess?" I smile at him.

"No, I don't have to guess, I know it was short, and it was the process. It's just that I don't know if the next time we'll succeed in doing it again."

"Oh, that! So now you want certainties in reality," I tease him. We both laugh.

"You are right, I forget my own medicine. I know that we can only learn or discover something new, building logical bridges from the current knowledge. And many times we must use our intuition and challenge our assumptions, but always building the logic." He raises his drink and says, "To the never ending learning."

"Salud amigo!"

"What about you? The news was promising in your last mail," Bill says changing the subject.

"Sales are growing, inventories are low, and profitability is extremely good —" Bill is not impressed and says, "Congratulations, but I want to know the real results."

I am confused; I thought I was telling him the results. As I stay quiet, he adds, "Do you remember someone that claimed to be contented but still...?" He smiles at me.

"Yes, we were doing well at that time but I was drowning in the urgent. You are right; those days are gone for me, and also for all the management team. We have a rule now; we turn the lights off at six. Everybody in the company looks happier."

"Now you are talking!" says Bill, "Don't you see that achieving that, financial results will follow? It is exactly what Goldratt says in that video that I sent you, his last public appearance in Baltimore, in April 2011."

"In that conversation, Goldratt remarks the fact that as long as the generic cloud is not eliminated, it will continue eroding human relationships in the company," I say recalling what I could relate to our case.

"Remember how we started?" Bill says, enjoying the moment.

"We started with a list of UDEs of my company. I remember that the consolidated cloud was not meaningful for me at first. Only when I could see a way out, I understood the full meaning of it." It's funny how I consider obvious now what I thought it was just blah, blah.

"And it was just a matter of eliminating the conflict with a breakthrough idea to build a decisive competitive edge." Bill says casually.

"Yeah, only that!" I say as we both laugh.

Bill is staring at me now, "What?" I ask.

"So you are leaving early every day now," he says and waits.

"You mean I could have more time with the family?" Bill nods. "Yes, and helping children with homework or having more time with Marcy is definitely one of the good results of using TOC," I say as I have this realization explicitly. "Now that I think of it, my family life has improved significantly lately, and I have to give all the credit to these actions that we have been executing guided by TOC."

"I'm very glad to hear that," he says. After a while, he asks, "When are you expanding capacity? Do you already know where and how much?" The relentless consultant is back.

"We haven't planned that yet. With the better flow in production we doubled our capacity. Don't worry, we didn't lay anybody off, I did as we discussed. We will need them all sooner or later, but we are far from doubling sales yet."

Bill studies my face and says, "What was the average sales growth during the last three months?"

"Average is five percent," I reply.

"Assuming that you don't grow any faster than that, how many months do you need to double sales at five per cent per month?"

"I guess twenty. Five times twenty is another hundred." I'm not following.

"People don't understand the exponential function. At five per cent you will double in fourteen months, three of which are already gone, so you have only eleven months to be ready with more capacity if you don't want to deteriorate the service. And considering that you need a twenty percent protective capacity because of the fluctuations, now you only have nine more months to get to the eighty percent level."

"If you are right we are late; only to decide specifications of the new machines and to ask for quotations we'll need three months." Bill is scaring me.

"And that is only growing at five percent," says Bill.

"Okay, I got it, back to the urgencies!" I knew it couldn't last for long.

"Don't be so dramatic. The worst thing that could happen now is that you will not expand sales for some months, 'stagnating' at double or triple of the market profitability. I wouldn't say you are in trouble," says Bill smiling.

"Besides," he adds, "this is the first competitive edge, and you need to stabilize all the processes to start thinking about the next one. But now it is not a firefighting mode of operation, but a real strategic planning and executing prudently only what you are pretty sure that will work, you will have the time to really check things out."

"It is a real process of ongoing improvement," I think aloud.

Bill nods and says, "That was the subtitle on the cover of 'The Goal'. Dr. Goldratt always thought in these terms, but his intuition and hard work, along with some mistakes, shaped the knowledge until very close to the last days he was with us; to the point that he finally claimed to have found the principles of the science of management."

"When you mentioned that, I did a search in YouTube, finding many different videos. Then I searched for 'science of management goldratt' and found exactly the video that you mentioned."

"Many claim to use scientific knowledge in management, and they do, but in a different sense, right?," says Bill. He is a little bit defensive now.

"I totally agree with you. I admit that it wouldn't have caught my attention before because there are so many people saying the same thing, that they really have a scientific approach to management."

Bill is very interested, "What is different now for you about TOC then?"

"The big difference is that I tried many approaches. And the four pillars and the tools provide a real framework that is generic and applicable to any organization. Now that I experienced it, I understand the inherent simplicity, and how all conflicts can be removed. And of course, 'never say I know' is something that opened new horizons for me."

"What about 'people are good'"? Bill says, as if checking.

"Even that was a refresher. I don't blame anyone anymore, that doesn't mean that everybody behaves aligned with the company. In the last two months we had to let go a few people because they couldn't adjust. They simply couldn't. We gave them all the opportunities, the training, the coaching. But we realized that the new way was not for them, and asking them to change put them in a conflict. They will be happier somewhere else, but I don't doubt that they are good."

"Yes, we in TOC never said that layoffs are forbidden. We only said that no company should let go anyone just to improve their bottom line."

Bill is just reinforcing what we discussed several times when capacity in production was revealed so suddenly, and I am reassured. I had pressure from the board to let go people, but I explained to them that it wouldn't be a smart move to lay off people that helped us improving. It wasn't that smooth but I prevailed.

"As you told me, loyalty is a two way street."

"I learned that from Goldratt," Bill says, not accepting the credit.

"I remember our first conversation when you started asking questions and using words like conflicts or fears. I can tell you now that I was on the verge of stopping everything because of those words."

"I noticed it and softened my language a little bit. What do you think about that now?"

"After watching that video several times, I fully understand how the clouds were the tools to deal with the fear of tug of war in the company. Even the concept of inherent simplicity was a clear way to deal with the fear of complexity. But I want to understand a little bit better how TOC helps dealing with the fear of uncertainty." I think that I understand but I want to listen what Bill's explanation is.

"Well, that is interesting, such as when you see so many efforts devoted just to somehow reduce uncertainty, like better forecasting systems."

As he drinks some wine I add, "I felt better when we bought that software for better forecasting, and now I see how wrong I was. It was just a mirage."

"The worst manifestation is the tendency to control everything, and by that interrupting the natural flow of things. For example, how was your production control before and how is it now?"

"Before we had the illusion of planning every single machine on the floor, knowing that those plans would change frequently. Now we know that we can't plan at that level, so the instructions are much simpler; only work when orders come to you and use the colors to decide priorities," I realize how obvious all this sounds to me now.

"And how do you decide what orders to release for work?"

"Now we only release work to keep our inventory buffers full," I say.

Bill then says, "You see, those buffers are there to absorb the uncertainty coming from demand fluctuations. Instead of trying to guess sales, TOC proposes to place buffers at the highest aggregation point possible."

"So instead of trying to be more precise than the noise, we just build buffers to be prepared for the uncertain; inventories, cash and protective capacity." I thought this was it, but I wanted to be sure that I wasn't missing anything.

"Mostly those, yes. The principle is to build a buffer whenever you are facing uncertainty. This principle was portrayed by Goldratt with the three rules of management: first rule is to be paranoid, second rule is to be paranoid," I laugh and say, "Third rule is to be paranoid?"

"No, third rule is not to be hysterical!," Bill laughs and seriously again adds, "Not being hysterical means to build the minimum buffer that gives you peace of mind. Being paranoid means to look at everything that is currently undesirable and find a good solution. But then, before implementing the solution, look at all the foreseeable risks of success, to be prepared and avoid them."

"Now I see clearly why you call TOC the science of management," I say.

"I would say that TOC is the practical application of science of management. I like to think of it as a methodology that allows managers to eliminate the sources of the urgent so they can really focus on the important," Bill reminds me of the first email message that started all.

"And it really does. By the way, Bill, I have told our board that you helped us during the last months and they approved the payment that I thought was only fair. I need you to send me an invoice for the amount that I transferred into your account just before this dinner, which is twenty per cent of the additional profit during the last quarter." I knew Bill wouldn't charge a cent and I didn't want to be a free rider, so I just made the payment before he could object.

"Thank you for that, it was not necessary at all, but it certainly helps," he says smiling. "You know what I really want you to do? Please, write something telling your story. Maybe it will be much better coming from a CEO."

"Okay, so you think that now I have time to write articles, don't you?" I tease him.

"Articles? What about a book?" Bill is always one step ahead.

"You know what; I've recorded all our meetings. I can write the introductory chapters and you do the rest," I say smiling back.

"Fair enough."

We finish our desserts and leave.

***

I drive Bill back home, because he came in a taxi. In the car, he gives me another surprise.

"To sustain and build more on top of what you have now, you need a tool for communication, synchronization and focus. We use for that the strategy and tactic trees, or S&T for short," he says just leaving.

"Is this another logical tree? I thought we had covered all the thinking process tools," I feel anxious with more complexity.

"It is a logical tool, it is used to organize all the knowledge in a hierarchical way, coming from the more general at the top, building the details in the various levels below," he says.

"Should I write one for us?," I want to know whether this would mean much more work for me.

"Oh, no. You just need a generic one that is already written, and we can discuss it to see whether it fits your company or it needs minor adaptations."

I'm relieved, and now I'm also interested in the synchronization thing. "You said this S&T tree is for communication and synchronization."

"And focusing," he adds, "to understand better this tool, we first need to define what strategy and what tactic are. Do you have any idea?" Bill asks. I learned that going through these questions is better than receiving only answers.

"Those are mostly military terms, but in business we use them to explain what the guiding ideas are. Strategy is the long term and high level objective and the way to achieve it. Tactics are low level and more detailed action plans."

"Not so far. Goldratt often told the story of how Einstein defined time, in order to explain his Theory of Relativity. Einstein said 'Time is the thing that is measured by a clock'," —says Bill. "Likewise, Eli had to first define strategy and tactic for use in his S&T trees, which he did this way: Strategy is defined as the answer to the question 'what for?' and tactic is the answer to the question 'how?'"

"Very simple and precise," I say.

"You see? You can answer those questions at every level of detail, so they come in pairs. The first strategy is always the same: to achieve a state where the company is generating more and more value to all its stakeholders; employees, clients and shareholders; in that order. In other words, sustainable and stable growth."

"Comparing to our situation five months back, I'd say that we are on the right track now." I like the definition and I can guess the tactic. "If I remember correctly, you mentioned the tactic when we were discussing our generic conflict. To build a decisive competitive edge, and the capabilities to capitalize on it, on big enough markets, without exhausting the company's resources and without taking real risks."

"Very good! I see you are a good student, as usual."

"As I told you, all our conversations are recorded and I review them frequently. Where can I get my generic tree?"

As I ask, Bill grabs his smart phone as he says, "I'm sending you and email with the website, http://www.harmonytoc.com, where you can register for free and download the Harmony viewer, which is a program to view written trees. It has a library with all the generic trees. You should look at the consumer goods tree."

"Well, you are a gentleman and a scholar. Thank you very much again," I say as I park in front of Bill's house.

"It was my pleasure. Don't forget to send me those recordings and your write up for the first chapters. Thanks for the ride, we'll speak again soon, bye."

"Sure, I'll be in touch."

XX

"What a pleasant surprise my friend, I thought you lived at your office," I am glad to see Tom again, it has been months since our last beer.

"You know how it is, we never get bored at work," Tom says as we order some beers and tartar with toasts.

"I wouldn't know, why don't you explain it to me?" I ask him casually.

"Come on! You surely have more fires to put out than me, after all I just have to decide whether I accept the orders or not. You must decide what to produce, guessing future demand."

Tom is right, my previous situation was surely worse than his, and now I don't have any emergencies at work.

"Tom, what do you think are the causes for your fires?" Tom looks surprised and says, "You are almost talking like Bill. Don't tell me that he brainwashed you!"

I laugh and remember how skeptic I was, too. "I've tried new things and they worked nicely for me. And yes, Bill helped me with some processes based on TOC. Why do you say that? Do you know what TOC is all about?"

"Bill tried to sell me once and he talked about trees and clouds. I didn't pay attention at that time because I didn't have the time for theoretical discussions. I did my research and saw that nobody that I know was talking about it."

I could have been looking at my old self in the mirror. If only Tom knew what I know now. "Tom, are you judging something based on what the majority is saying?"

"It is definitely a way to do it, otherwise I wouldn't have time to do anything else but examine every new management theory in detail."

"Would you take my word that it is worth trying a full session?"

"So you are serious, what results did you get?"

"Good enough results to advise you to try." So the inside lock is hard to open after all.

"I will think about it."

* * *

"Bill, hi, I'm calling you because I need your help with Tom. We had an informal discussion and he admitted to have plenty of fires at work. I believe he is drowning in the urgent. When do you think you could have a first session with him?"

"Richard, I'm very glad that you called me for this. I don't want to do it." This was unexpected as it pulled the rug from under my feet.

"What do you mean? You don't want to help Tom?" I can't believe it.

"On the contrary. Richard, you are a much better candidate to help him, after all what you went through." Bill sounds serious.

"I don't have the experience or the knowledge!" I try to protest.

"Really? Who is training all your internal teams?"

"I am, but this is different," I really don't think this is a good idea.

"You've got all the recordings, and the experience of what happened in your case, and you've been improving dramatically in the last months in your TOC skills. Don't look for excuses."

I ran out of excuses.

"Besides," says Bill, "when you give knowledge, you receive more knowledge. Do it for yourself."

"So you don't want to help," I give it my last shot.

"I didn't say that, Richard. I will always be available. However, you don't know your capabilities at present, do you? What do you think is the limit for you?"

"I guess that not even the sky is the limit," I say with a smile.

"Very good, the last phrase of 'Isn't it Obvious?', and most appropriate."

"Okay, I will do it."

"Richard, please don't forget the write up for the first chapters, now that I agreed to write your book, I need your collaboration."

XXI

"Thank you for making this time slot in your tight agenda," I know how Tom should feel about my insistence on discussing his problems from the Goldratt Theory perspective.

"On the contrary, thank you for coming. I am surprised that you could spend this time."

"Look Tom, if I couldn't come for a meeting with you, I would be in deep trouble."

"Why is that? But before you answer, a coffee, a soda?"

"Just water for me, thanks." As Tom asks for water and a tea, I try to organize my thoughts in a good and precise phrase.

"If I don't have spare time it only means that I can't do everything that I must do." I learned this lesson the hard way.

"But surely there are always things to use your time with at the office, right?"

"Of course, I can always find something to do! That doesn't mean that I should do it." I catch a funny glance from Tom.

"What?"

"Listen, I have learned that focus is the key word." I wait while these words sink in Tom's mind.

"Of course, that is obvious. I think that I am focusing my attention in getting the best possible results."

"Do you?" Maybe Tom's inside lock is double, I will try provoking him a little bit.

"What do you mean? Of course I am!"

"You have told me enough for me to guess some facts in your company. Do you want to hear my conclusions?" If he doesn't, I learned that it is better to wait. By now I expect at least curiosity.

"Go ahead, wizard."

"As you told me that there many things in your to-do list, at the extent that you cannot finish everything every day, I would say that you face many urgent issues." I want to start safe.

"Yes, what's the guess? This is what all general managers are facing, aren't they?" I will not fall in the trap of diverting the conversation to bitching and moaning.

"Thanks, and from that I can conclude that you have to deal with many internal conflicts, like between sales and production, or sales and finance, or finance and logistics." As I say this I can sense how Tom grows impatient.

"Is there anything new in your conclusions? Because, I haven't seen the light so far." Good, I remember that 'obvious' is the best compliment for a good reasoning.

"My claim is that eliminating all those internal conflicts, your company will have such harmony that financial results will come as a logical derivation." Before he can jump in, I rush to add, "And as long as all those conflicts exist, you will be trapped in the urgent, working very hard for just an average result." Now I expect some reaction, but surprisingly Tom is in deep thought. I wait. Eventually Tom speaks again but in a softer tone of voice, as if he is revealing a secret.

"You may think that now I would consider all that as soft and unimportant. However, you reminded me of a seminar that I attended two years ago about Stephen Covey's theory; you know the book, 'The seven habits of highly effective people'."

"I do, very good book and very aligned with what I was saying."

"Exactly! And after that seminar I thought of training all our people. We did some efforts, and we got some results, too. But conflicts came again, and I know I can't blame my people but I don't know why we should have these training sessions every six months just to come back to square one every time."

"I didn't know that you had that clarity about the real problem. I didn't have it myself when I started. For you then, it is much better than I thought." Tom is quiet and waiting as if knowing that good news are coming.

"What I have learned in the last six months is that Goldratt Theory is all about people. It is about developing people unleashing their true potential, and it is about improving significantly human relationships in the company." This realization refreshes my mind as the water refreshes my throat with the last drink. Tom looks hesitant.

"I thought all that TOC thing was about improving productivity."

"It is, but productivity is a much wider and deeper concept for me now. The meaning of eliminating the internal conflicts is way beyond just creating peace by compromising. It is about creating a situation where suppliers and clients are very satisfied with their relationship with the company, which in turn is only a reflection of much better harmony within the company. In such a situation, financial results will come as a consequence for sure." I even mimicked the tone of voice with which Eli used in his last public appearance in Baltimore saying this same thing.

"If I didn't know, I would have said that you were selling me. But I know what problems you had in the past and I believe that it is worth exploring more what apparently worked so nicely for you." Wow!, at last. First layer is behind; let us now move forward to agree on the direction, but not today.

"We've just started. I am now building more and more the capabilities of my people. We are learning how to turn all the 'engines of disharmony' into engines of harmony." When I say this I realize that it sounded like mumbo jumbo and I study Tom's face.

"I don't know much about TOC jargon. Can you tell me a little bit more about those engines?" Well, Tom took it the best way possible, and now I will just tell him what I know, which is the same as saying, not much.

"I'm just learning all this, and this is not the first thing to do. When we start the analysis, you will see that the focus will be on very practical things, like improving your due date performance and reducing your lead times," I say and Tom interrupts me.

"That sounds great! I'd be delighted only with those two." He smiles for the first time in a while.

"I bet you would!," it is good that we can relax again. "But I can give you some highlights about those engines as Dr. Goldratt called them." I drink more water, gaining valuable seconds to think before speaking again.

"One thing that causes disharmony is the misalignment between authority and responsibility," as Tom makes a face, I disregard it saying, "don't worry, you will see this is real. And we now use a tool to detect and correct all those misalignments." Tom is listening attentively, as quenching a thirst that was also mine months ago.

"Other sources for disharmony are both not knowing how I contribute to the company and not knowing how others contribute to the company." Again a face of surprise. "Tom, as CEOs we don't realize to what extent, people at the lower levels of the company are in this situation. The fact that we can answer these questions easily doesn't mean that everybody else can also. But giving them the why's of the things they do, we start relying more on really empowered people. They grow with TOC as they start thinking more clearly instead of just following instructions." I don't think Tom understands everything, but he asked for it.

"I have seen that by empowering people and focusing everybody on one single big initiative, we, the management team, have released time and have increased our capacity." Probably he doesn't understand now the meaning of elevating the constraint, but he will.

"Inertia is another thing that could be in the way. But now, with people really thinking, we are alert to change procedures when conditions change. And of course, we introduced and are using more and more the thinking tools to evaporate clouds of conflicts."

"What? Evaporate what things?" Tom's face is now really puzzled.

"Don't worry. You will see how simple everything is. For now, I can tell you only this. And we need a first session of three hours without interruptions to start."

"Three hours!," as he says this I smile at him remembering my own reaction with the first request from Bill. "I can do it next Wednesday in the morning, could you do it then?," he says looking at his laptop.

"Perfect, I will be here."

XXII

"Come on!, don't overreact, Richard", Tom is pacing up and down my office when Bill shows up. We called him just an hour ago when our discussion diverted to philosophical depths.

"What is this joker telling you?" Bill comes in and helps himself a bottle of water while he looks amused by the scene.

"I was telling Tom that all this stuff about Goldratt Theory and the science of management made me wonder whether we could say that Goldratt really built a simple formulation to manage organizations." I can't hide my excitement and Bill is now also surprised.

"What do you mean? Goldratt Theory is based on the concept of inherent simplicity contained in any system or organization. Are you implying something deeper?" Bill is cautious and I learned that he wouldn't claim something based on only speculation.

"Look, after two months of implementing some ideas, Tom has already solved most of his problems, sorry, undesirable effects. He is now very close to delivering 100% on time whereas all the competition is at 80% or less. Now it's clear that remarkably reliable delivery is a significant need of his markets. So he has built a decisive competitive edge having achieved such performance. Today we are going to think of how to capitalize on such a fantastic advantage."

Bill is not surprised with all this. No wonder; he sent me the generic strategies and tactics tree that would fit for Tom's company. As he seems not to understand, I continue.

"Don't you see? I could solve most of my problems in weeks with very simple ideas. Now, Tom could do the same in weeks again. I've been thinking that these are not isolated cases."

Now, Bill starts to look excited. "And considering all the years that you and Tom have been trying to solve the same problems, trying many different approaches, with very limited success as you both told me, you think that TOC is special."

"I believe that TOC is more than special. I watched again that video on YouTube about the science of management and probably Goldratt found the three variables that need to be managed in any organization: flow, uncertainty and human relationships. Not only that, he found the simple formulation by which the three of them are related…"

"… And now, we have the principles to manage any organization in a very simple way!" Bill jumped as if waking up. "What you did in your company is just an application of these simple principles. Now, Tom is using another application of the same principles. Amazing!" Bill's head is now at full speed, I can tell.

"I hate interrupting such a fascinating dialog," Tom says, "but we need to develop some things here, like an offer and how to sell it, remember?"

"Of course, it is just that a realization like this could change management discipline for good", I say.

"You are right, Richard, it is so important that we need to devote enough time and effort to formally understand what is wrong in the former management theories, which clearly haven't solved the organizational problems that you both have successfully eliminated in such a short time."

"Fine, it is settled. Let us schedule some working sessions for that later. Let's focus now on Tom's case." As I say this, both nod and Tom shows an ample smile for he has two good friends working for him.

I'm sure that we both will do much better in the future, and I also know that this is just the beginning.

www.ingramcontent.com/pod-product-compliance
Lightning Source LLC
Chambersburg PA
CBHW051523170526
45165CB00002B/585